# Upstate Down

*Thinking about New York and its Discontents*

**Alexander R. Thomas and Polly J. Smith**

**University Press of America,® Inc.**
**Lanham · Boulder · New York · Toronto · Plymouth, UK**

**University Press of America,® Inc.**
4501 Forbes Boulevard
Suite 200
Lanham, Maryland 20706
UPA Acquisitions Department (301) 459-3366

Estover Road
Plymouth PL6 7PY
United Kingdom


Printed in the United States of America
British Library Cataloging in Publication Information Available

Library of Congress Control Number: 2008941643
ISBN-13: 978-0-7618-4499-0 (clothbound : alk. paper)
ISBN-13: 978-0-7618-4500-3 (paperback : alk. paper)
eISBN13: 978-0-7618-4501-0

™ The paper used in this publication meets the minimum requirements of American National Standard for Information Sciences—Permanence of Paper for Printed Library Materials, ANSI Z39.48—1984

*For*

Robert, Todd & Lindsay

*The Sources of Joy in our Lives*

# Contents

# List of Tables

# List of Figures

# Preface

The Olympics began today. The whole world is aflutter with the marvels of Beijing and our children dream of Olympic glory in the pool. The television pans across sweeping views of a transformed urban landscape, and we fantasize of an international games spread across both sides of the river in Niagara Falls. Picture Olympic divers flying through the air with the falls as their background; it would be a view to rival Barcelona. Or runners winding their way through by the sheer cliffs by the river, or simply the spectacle of the first Olympic games to be hosted by two countries simultaneously. Alas, it seems to be fantasy, for who in New York dreams such big dreams anymore?

As members of the motley cohort called Generation X, we grew up in the world after the Moon Landings and oil shocks. Ours is a transitional generation that was exposed to the expectations of progress shared with the previous generation and the rigid acknowledgment of limits borne of stagflation. We can dream of getting on a train in Utica's Union Station and arriving in Grand Central Station an hour and a half later. We can picture the artist studios and cafes lining the streets in Utica's oldest neighborhood of converted warehouses and new apartments revived by high speed rail, but we also know the reality that few are calling for such a radical vision. We can also picture bringing our children to an aquarium in Albany – smaller cities have them, so why not? – and an educational system this is active, even fanatic, about creating positive change in New York's communities. And a health care system so good that retirees don't even think of leaving New York behind. But we also feel boxed in by the politics of limitation. There's no money; we must compete in a global marketplace against places with lower taxes and wages; we're past our prime. We know. But we also know that such thinking reproduces the same conditions, and the results are not good. If we want to live in a strong and healthy New York, we need to change our thinking.

This work is not an academic treatise, nor is there a plan to get from point A to point B. We are simply a husband and wife team of sociologists who believe that New York can compete, but we need to change the terms under which we compete. We advocate thinking about policy holistically, stressing not only the economy, but the environment and culture and, especially, politics. Only through a concerted effort to diagnose New York's problems can we formulate policies to combat New York's ills, and this requires a new way of thinking.

We should thank Bill Wilkerson and Brian Lowe at SUNY College at Oneonta for enduring conversations with us about New York's woes, and Jan DeAmicis at Utica College for doing the same. The staff at Milne Library at SUNY Oneonta has been helpful as always. Robert and Todd should also be commended for once again enduring "the book" with no complaints. Robert Smith has provided valuable feedback, as have the anonymous reviewers.

The research in this book was made possible by the generosity of a Walter B. Ford Research Grant from SUNY College at Oneonta.

Alexander R. Thomas
Polly J. Smith
Utica, N. Y.
8 August 2008

# Hadrian's Wall 1

In the year 117 the Roman Emperor Hadrian came to power. His predecessor, Trajan, had expanded the boundaries of his empire to the greatest extent ever to be enjoyed by Rome. Perhaps Trajan knew that the empire would grow no more, but it seems unlikely. Only in hindsight could one know that Rome had peaked, and that the plan of Hadrian was to proclaim "good enough" and draw the lines where the armies made camp. In Britain, the monument to the peak of the Roman Empire winds its way across the countryside and is appropriately known as "Hadrian's Wall." The wisdom of Hadrian's policy is open to debate: was it an enlightened acknowledgement of the limits of Roman power, or merely an expression of the politics of limitation? In any case, New York finds itself at a similar crossroads. In the years following World War II New York was home to a booming economy and a prosperous workforce; the future appeared bright as nearly every city in the state had witnessed decades of continuous population growth. Cities were aging but still strong and suburbs were booming; rural communities still formed the backbone of the largest industry in the state: agriculture. A few decades later and we are left to ask: was that the peak? Or are we experiencing a temporary downturn?

The Empire State is in a malaise. In cities and suburbs across upstate people are moving elsewhere, choosing to leave after jobs do the same. Most often, they opt to start new lives in other states because their jobs have left the country entirely or, in many cases, no longer exist at all. In Cortland, county officials are rebuilding after Smith Corona moved its manufacturing operations to Mexico. In Schenectady, a sea of parking fields has replaced buildings at the sprawling General Electric campus. In Buffalo, every census seems to bring more bad news as residents flee a city that epitomizes deindustrialization. As the population growth rate is anemic statewide, closer examination reveals a downstate keeping pace with the national average as upstate bleeds people and business. And in Albany, politicians acknowledge the problem but then roll out new twists on old policy designs: lower taxes, subsidies to business and communities, and, one presumes, prayer. Beyond the well-advertised exceptions, such policies are not working.

Why should we be concerned about the trends found in the state of New York today? Well, the humanitarian reasons come to mind, but as social scientists there is another reason as well: as New York goes, so goes the rest of the country. Simply stated, throughout much of American history, trends witnessed in New York have later been found in the rest of the nation. With its vast interior, New York was one of the first frontier states, with the "Wild West" pushing through the state as early as the 1780s and 1790s. In the early nineteenth century there were massive expenditures for roads and, of course, the Erie Canal. By the 1830s there were railroads—all of which would be built later in much of the rest of the country. Not surprisingly, New York was one of the earliest states to meet the industrial revolution, with textile mills in New York Mills as early as 1808 (Pula & Dziedzic, 2005). The shift to high technology occurred first in New York with such nineteenth century wonders as photography in Rochester and electricity in Schenectady and Niagara Falls. With such industrial prowess, New York was also at the forefront for social movements to increase social equality, with the women's rights movement beginning in Seneca Falls (hence, the Seneca Falls Movement), abolitionist and civil rights movements in Rochester, and the labor movement winning big gains in large cities like New York and small cities like Oneonta.

Does this really mean that as New York goes there goes the nation? Not necessarily—if social scientists were so good at making predictions none of us would be working anymore. But it is a trend to which we should perhaps pay close attention. As the twentieth century went on, New York was among the first states to invest heavily in the car, building such highways as the Bronx River Parkway (public) and Motor Parkway (private) decades before interstates to help motorists escape the city, and not surprisingly New York was one of the first states to experience significant suburbanization and inner city decline. As a consequence, New York cities were among the first to experiment with large scale urban renewal—again, decades before the federal programs of the Fifties and Sixties—with the same rather dismal consequences seen nationwide. New York was also one of the first states to see entire metropolitan areas devastated by the flight of manufacturing, the dubious distinction going to Utica's textile industry and Buffalo's steel industry. Such industrial flight is today part of the conventional wisdom as such terms as "NAFTA" and "GATT" have entered the lexicon of common citizens normally uninspired by the details of trade agreements and other international treaties. At the time of upstate's undoing, however, such trends appeared novel and seemed to be little more than episodic downturns in an otherwise healthy economy. Today, not just business but also people leave the state.

All news is not necessarily bad, however. It is possible that New York can once again be the first to address new problems and trends. While it is true that civilizations grow and eventually die, it is too early to write off the Empire State. But to address our woes, it is necessary to step back and take a fresh look at what is happening.

## An Outsider's Perspective

There are advantages to being political insiders. There is a clarity about the true politics of the state. For instance, in 2008 we were approached by a student who wished to go to law school. Although she had a substantial financial aid package from a law school in New England, she was advised by a capital district attorney (and aunt) that if she wished to work in state government she would be better off attending Albany Law School. That is useful information that will not appear in a guidebook. But such insider status may also unduly commit one to the status quo—a reluctance to challenge the current system even if it seems to be outdated. As such, we do not advocate either an "insiders" or an "outsiders" perspective. It is important that both perspectives be incorporated into policy. What we are presenting in this analysis is an "outsider" perspective.

We are a husband and wife team of sociologists—one at a small private college and the other in the grey concrete towers of SUNY. We do not claim to have the answers, but we can share a perspective with widespread acceptance among the social sciences. Our goal is merely to add to the ongoing discussion about upstate New York.

Any society can be described as a "complex system." That is to say that the number of variables that inform any event are often too numerous to be precisely known—each aspect of a person's personality, for instance, can be an important variable; or perhaps not. Certain variables are generally more important than others, however, and because of this can be used to describe how a society operates. There are many ways of describing the basic elements of society, and ours is not necessarily better than the schemes of others. But our scheme helps us in our analyses, and is adapted from that of the great sociologists Talcott Parsons (1951) and Michael Mann (1986; see also Thomas, 2005).

A society is not only a complex system, but it is a continually evolving system. Actually, that is in part what it means to be a complex system. Because it is constantly evolving, a stable state is not achievable (you can't stop time), and so the "equilibrium" of economy mythology is not truly possible. If things seem perfect the way they are—watch out! If you are not completely satisfied, keep in mind that things could get better; or worse. In any case, society is too vague a concept at this point, so we should say that the social life of people in a population evolves within the confines of, or rather is guided by, four basic institutions rooted in individual human nature and thus common to all societies: polity, economy, culture and environment.

All humans must on occasion make a decision. Even in our most remote past, decisions needed to be made and these often had a connection with other parameters of life. Twenty-thousand years ago one might have thought about food and said to oneself, "Today, should I pick berries or attempt to kill a boar?" Add a few compatriots and there is a need for group-level decision making, and blow up the scale by 18 million and you have New York State politics. Polity is often dominated by the individual pursuit of power, but also includes such concepts as ideology and sheer brutal force. For our own purposes, it reflects the interaction of individual "players" in state government—both elected and not. Polity often influences what policies are and are not possible, and by doing so often influences what people even imagine as possible. During the early and mid-twentieth century, the idea of building expressways from one end of the nation to the other was politically possible. Today, even though as a nation we are far more wealthy, the interstate highway system could not only not pass Congress, but few would spend their time even thinking about such a far-flung idea.

Polity is often intimately—far more than the elite often wants to admit—tied to the economy. As Kevin Phillips (2003) demonstrated, nearly all the great fortunes of the past one thousand years were due at least in part to tight connections with government. When we moderns think of the economy we think of the stock market and interest rates, but from a social science perspective an economy is the system developed to ensure that the basic human needs—food, water, shelter, clothing, even sex—are met. As basic as the economy is, it is tempting to think that it is the most important component of a society, but it is not. Ultimately, a shift in the environment can (and has) wiped out entire communities, and polity and education (a function of culture) are critical to the functioning of an economy. Nevertheless, as with the others, if the economy does not function then the society will falter. As we discuss in chapter two, although there might be something to be desired in New York's climate, it is not ultimately responsible for people leaving the state—it is often the economy that must shoulder that burden. Nevertheless, while the economy is sometimes treated as the most important component of a society, the same tangle of institutional interdependencies that exist for other aspects of society exist for the economy as well. For instance, the overall level of education is related to what types of industries can be supported. Similarly, even a great idea for a store or restaurant can fail if it does not respect the cultural practices and tastes of its customer base.

Culture is not really a fine wine or expensive art, although these are expressions of culture. Properly speaking, culture is the accumulation of knowledge common to members of a society. This includes technology, tastes, and the educational process of passing this knowledge to new people. Just as polity and economy can establish what is and is not possible or feasible, culture plays a substantial role as well. In short, in the matter of policy it determines how ideas are treated: as fantasy or as realistic goal, or somewhere in between. When boosters forwarded the idea of the Erie Canal, the culture allowed for such a flight of creative fancy in the form of public works projects. This is true of the time of the building of the Interstate Highway System as well. It is not merely that politicians of the time were willing to go ahead with such projects; it is also that the culture allowed for such projects to be dreamt up and considered desirable. Today, in contrast, our culture is best described by what Max Weber (1947) called "rationalization" and C. Wright Mills (1959) called "Abstract Empiricism." Our culture is highly bureaucratized and emphasizes the establishment of "proof" and measurement of what is possible and what is not. We employ vast bureaucracies to manage the status quo, and as a consequence we tend to define innovation as a mere extension of the status quo. Gone are the days of big ideas and risk-taking behavior—if it doesn't pay off in five years, it's not worth it. Let them do it in the Carolinas! The idea of a massive network of highways would likely not be possible today, and certainly few are proposing new ideas that rival the Erie Canal in its audaciousness or its potential impact.

Much has been made of the state of the environment in recent years, and rightly so. All societies are ultimately subject to the whims of the environment, and environmental damage has contributed to the demise of such great civilizations as the Maya and the Babylonians. Environment, however, refers to more than just climate—the human-made environment often influences us in unseen ways. For instance, residents of New York City often walk more than suburbanites, and this might influence rates of heart disease. More in social science phenomena, the automobile contributes to a lifestyle where people go great distances for work, shopping, and entertainment. It enables the creation of an extensive tourism industry based on the car. But it has also provided the death blow for downtown areas all over the state and nation. It is a technology that has spawned an environment of houses on large lots set considerable distances from other people—an environment where it is not uncommon that people do not know their neighbors.

All of these aspects of society are intimately intertwined—it is not possible to separate one from another. All too often, however, we seek a "magic bullet" to turn things around—Empire Zones to give business the tax advantages of companies in Alabama, for instance, to revitalize the economy. Certainly, they work for those companies that have located in them, but they have hardly revitalized a state whose problems are more deeply rooted. Or consider the beautification of downtown areas in an attempt to return them to their former glory. The results are often mixed as some communities are able to capitalize on such programs but others do not. The remainder of this book will examine a number of communities and assess recent trends with the above framework. At times, we will propose policies based on our social scientific assessment—diagnosis, if you will. We'll leave it to you to assess how viable these ideas actually are.

## The Rest of the Book

In chapter two, we examine recent trends affecting New York, particularly upstate New York. We look first at the image popularly attributed to upstate communities and how it relates to reality. We often think of upstate as "rural," even though most upstate residents live in metropolitan areas. We then examine how each of the major areas of the state have performed in terms of population growth or decline. Although there are numerous ways to study the relative health of cities and regions, population change is ultimately the most credible: if a region is attracting large numbers of migrants, things are likely going well. If a region is losing population, it is because people are looking for a way to get out. We then examine the "four myths of upstate decline" often cited by New Yorkers for why New York seems to be past its prime.

In chapter three, we examine the impact of what was arguably the most successful policy decision in New York history: the building of the Erie Canal. The canal had a great impact on New York, and it did so by utilizing a favorable natural environment (it was a good place to build a canal) by altering the built environment (the canal was actually built). Debated for decades, the Erie Canal was the latest of several attempts to build a water route from the Hudson Valley to the Great Lakes, either Lake Ontario or Lake Erie. Once started, engineers built the first segments in relatively flat areas so that progress was swift and critics could be disarmed. Once completed, the shipping of freight through the canal system helped turn New York City into the largest port in America and Buffalo one of the largest on the Great Lakes. The cities that grew along its route became the high technology centers of their day, and together they formed the Empire State.

In chapters four through six, we examine recent trends in New York by discussing several case studies that illustrate larger issues affecting the state. In chapter four, we continue to look at issues related to the built environment by examining the physical restructuring of metropolitan areas and smaller communities in New York State, paying particular attention to transportation. In chapter five, we examine the economy in New York by tracing the experience of several communities in upstate New York, particularly Buffalo and Rochester, Utica, Oneonta and Little Falls. In chapter six, we turn our attention to cultural resources and education.

In chapter seven we examine the plans recently forwarded by both parties for reviving upstate New York. We find the plans to be rather similar in that neither party has proffered ideas that break from the past. In each case, ideas such as lowering taxes or building infrastructure are offered with sketchy details about how to pay. In chapter eight, we discuss the issue of New York being a donor state, followed by our own ideas for restructuring state and local government in a way that would dramatically alter the fiscal demands of government and enhance responsiveness to local residents. In chapter nine, we revisit the themes discussed in this chapter and conclude the book.

# New York State of Mind 2

It's one of the "bluest" places in the nation. Its streets are lined with boutiques and cafes attended by hip college students, artists, and upwardly mobile professionals. It receives millions of dollars every year in federal and state money through its various institutions, and that money attracts the best and the brightest from around the world to work on exciting research projects, *avant garde* sculptures and paintings, and perhaps start new companies to sell their wares around the world. The city has culture and all that goes with it—good food, the arts, and attractive people. It has been called among the best places in the nation to live, and many residents are rightfully proud of its quality of life. It is, of course, Ithaca. Okay, some of you might have been thinking of that other bastion of liberal politics—New York City.

New York State is an enigma. Among the most loyal "blue states," it is in reality an amalgam of competing interests, ethnic and racial groups, religious convictions, and political ideologies. It defies easy explanation, no matter how we may try. Ithaca's Tompkins County went for John Kerry in 2004 because of the presence of Cornell University, right? Perhaps, but why did Kingston's Ulster County do the same? These are not big cities, but they are not rural counties either. Well, that explanation helps, too—such rural counties as Hamilton and Steuben shine as red as a stop light, but a look across state lines shows us that Berkshire County, Massachusetts, is actually bluer than Springfield's Hampden County right next door. In reality, except for the handful of bright blue or fiery red counties, New York is rather purple. Long Island is purple, central New York is purple, the Canadian border is purple. Different shades, perhaps, but purple just the same.

Such diversity in politics mirrors the complexity found throughout the state. We often hear that New York is in trouble, but that depends on where and who you are. Some places in New York have seen almost continual population decline for over thirty years; in others, the problem is rapid growth and sprawl. Large swaths of the state simply stagnate. The various layers of government found in New York confuse even those who work in government, and the best description of the electorate's response to the on-time budget of 2005 was, after over a decade of no such luck, quiet shock.

Within this mess is the region we call "upstate." Containing the vast majority of the state's land area but less than half the population, we have a tendency to discuss state politics as an "upstate/downstate" struggle. However, the reality is more complex. A 2003 Brookings Institute report called upstate—which they defined as those counties north of the New York Metropolitan Area—the nation's "third slowest growing 'state'" (Pendall, 2003). Upstate grew slower than every state except West Virginia and North Dakota—and both are considerably more rural than upstate. During the 1990s, things got very bad as more people moved out of upstate than into upstate—they tended to go either to other northeastern states or to the south (Pendall, 2003). One group that grew was college students, but only while they were in college—at graduation they moved (Pendall et al, 2004). Another group that grew was the prison population, accounting for thirty percent of new upstate residents during the 1990s (Pendall, 2003). Not surprisingly, "personal income in Upstate grew at just half the national rate in the 1990s, and by 2000 lagged the country by 11 percent" (Pendall & Christopherson, 2004, 3). There are, however, large areas of downstate facing persistent crisis, such as the swath of poverty stretching from northern Manhattan into the Bronx, or persistent issues of urban decay in some older suburbs. Similarly, upstate has some areas that do grow, such as the Albany suburbs and greater Ithaca. Nevertheless, there is a general "upstate/downstate" flavor to the issue, and if such disparities are allowed to continue, they will have a profound effect on the culture and politics of New York State.

In fact, besides different economic fortunes, the main difference between the two regions is perhaps our relative familiarity of each. Scan the channels with your remote control, and a variety of television shows focus on or are broadcast from New York City: Law & Order, CSI New York, Seinfeld, Law & Order, the Today Show, every network news broadcast, MTV's Total Request Live, Law & Order—you get the picture. Plus there are numerous movies, songs, plays, musicals—even video games—that put New York in the spotlight. But our friends upstate might want to recognize that the lens frequently does not extend very far from the city limits, and that even folks in Westchester County and Long Island might feel a little excluded by comparison. That said, what happens when the media lens does turn north?

## Image?

It was 1997, and a new situation comedy aired on NBC that featured an upstate city—sort of. The show was called *Jenny*, after its star, MTV VJ and Sex Goddess Jenny McCarthy. Jenny played an upstate girl who grew up in Utica. With about 300 thousand residents, the Utica metropolitan area is larger than over half of the metropolitan areas in the United States; it fares poorly by New

York standards, however, and is only the seventh largest in the State. In the first episode, Uticans dropped their mouths as Jenny complained of her hum-drum life in Utica and asks a friend and fellow cashier, "What is it about Utica that grows a man's butt?" Luckily, a twist of fate—the death of Jenny's estranged father—helps the two young women move to Los Angeles, where a lawyer advises them to, "go back to your little burg; marry a couple of nice local boys named Buck and Bo; join a bowling league; and start poppin' out babies, because this town will swallow you whole" (Thomas, 2003, 122). In a later episode, Jenny decides to have her tongue pierced, because, "it's about as far from Utica as you can get; no one back there has their tongue pierced...our days as small town dorks are over" (Thomas, 2003, 123). Utica—like the larger upstate region of which it is a part—was portrayed as a place to leave and those left behind were to be pittied. The city was used as a symbol of small town life, to the disgust of Uticans and the dismay of people who really do live in small towns. NBC pulled the series before the end of the season, but not because portraying upstate New York as a bad stereotype is out of fashion; indeed, misleading portrayals of upstate New York are quite common.

For other misleading portrayals of upstate, one needs to look no further than the New York State Museum and Library. There is a considerable display about New York City, including a genuine subway car and historic maps. There is also an Adirondack logging camp, an Iroquois longhouse, and mannequins of the hunter/gatherer groups that lived in New York during the Ice Age. Curiously, there is relatively little about the Erie Canal. With little about the canal, there is also very little about the great canal cities: Utica, Syracuse, Rochester & Buffalo. There is almost nothing about smaller communities in the state, like Oneonta, Batavia, Jamestown, or Ogdensburg. There was, at one point, an interesting story of a railroad line in Elmira, but nothing of note about Binghamton. There are, however, lots of bugs pinned to display cases and stuffed bird carcasses. It is a fitting tribute not to the Empire State, but rather to the way we increasingly think of it: New York City, the Adirondack play land, and those nasty places in between.

And if the State Museum doesn't convince you that we're forgetting a lot of land and people, take a look at the license plate. New York, it reads, flanked on either side by the New York City skyline and Niagara Falls. Why not the Rochester skyline? Or even the Buffalo skyline? Utica has a skyline, and even a model of it in Hanna Park. Yes, one might say that New York City and Niagara Falls are "symbols" of New York, but that's a cop-out. We choose symbols based, to some degree anyway, on what we want to believe about ourselves. The New York City skyline is a symbol of urban greatness, of a thriving economy that extends all over the world. And Niagara Falls is a tremendous natural wonder. Of course we should be proud of them. Nevertheless, we also ignore symbols of failure. That New York skyline appears to be below 110$^{th}$ Street, for instance. It's Niagara Falls, the natural wonder, not Niagara Falls, the city. And to some degree, our selective vision of New York State is indicative of the conditions found in the state.

When we discuss "upstate," the imagery is most often of the countryside. Kramer and Elaine steal a dog on the sitcom *Seinfeld*, and drop it off upstate to "be in the country." Our tourism marketing shows a vibrant and exciting Manhattan, and contrasts the serenity of a drive near Cooperstown or the fresh air of a Lake Placid ski lift. But most in upstate New York do not live in such places, but rather in the other relatively large metropolitan areas. (A metropolitan area is a central city and its suburban county or counties). In fact, overshadowed though they are by New York, Philadelphia, and Boston, upstate New York cities are often large enough to be the largest cities of other states. For instance, the Buffalo-Niagara Falls area, including the cross-bridge traffic from Ontario, is comparable in size to metropolitan Pittsburgh and larger than the metropolitan areas of such cities as New Orleans and Salt Lake City. Actually, both those metropolitan areas are smaller than the Rochester and Albany metropolitan areas as well.

## New York: The Real Picture

New York State is a region that straddles two great cultural regions of the United States. Downstate is the heart of a dense urban agglomeration that stretches from the western suburbs of Wilmington, Delaware to the northern reaches of Springfield, Massachusetts. That is, it is solidly urbanized between these metropolitan areas, and New York City is one of several, and arguably the most important, urban centers in this largest of American "megalopolises." Containing not only the New York Metropolitan Area, but also the Philadelphia, New Haven, Hartford, and Springfield Metropolitan Areas as well, this region was home to nearly 29 million residents, nearly ten percent of America's population, in 2007—more than the next two largest North American megalopolises, Mexico City (18 million) and Los Angeles-San Diego (17 million). And that does not include the Washington-Baltimore and Boston metropolitan areas!

Upstate is often characterized as "rural," and much of the landscape is rural, but the population is not. Upstate is characterized by what geographers in the past called the "urban streak" of metropolitan areas along the route of the Erie Canal. On the basis of commuting patterns, settlement patterns, and media markets, we identify four major urban regions along the canal corridor: Buffalo-Niagara Falls, Rochester, Syracuse-Utica, and the Capital District centered on Albany. Each of these regions has a certain degree of economic and cultural integration, and each contains over a million residents. Any one of them would be the largest urban agglomeration in such states as South Carolina, Maine, Mississippi, Iowa, or Wyoming (whose population would be over tripled). On either side of this corridor is a more rural region that nonetheless is still heavily influ-

**Table 2.1:** Urban Regions in New York State, their Component Metropolitan and Micropolitan Areas, and Population Change, 1990-2007

| Urban Region | 1990 Population | 2007 Population | Change (%) | Component MA/ CSA[1] |
|---|---|---|---|---|
| New York | 19,710,239 | 21,961,994 | 2,251,755 (11.4) | New York CSA |
| Buffalo-Ste. Cathe-rines-Niagara[2] | 1,638,074 | 1,598,587 | -39,287 (-2.5) | Saint Catherine's-Niagara MA, Buffa-lo-Niagara Falls CSA |
| Rochester-Batavia-Seneca Falls | 1,096,153 | 1,122,845 | 26,963 (2.1) | Rochester, Batavia, Seneca Falls CSA |
| Albany-Glens Falls-Amsterdam | 1,097,136 | 1,148,416 | 51,280 (4.5) | Albany-Schenectady- Ams-terdam CSA |
| Syracuse-Utica-Auburn | 1,058,810 | 1,020,221 | -38,589 (-3.7) | Syracuse-Auburn CSA, Utica-Rome MA |

[1] MA designates areas defined as Metropolitan Areas by United States or Canadian Census Bureau; CSA designates region defined as a Combined Statistical Area by the United States Census Bureau—these roughly correspond to what in previous iterations of the Census were called Combined Statistical Metropolitan Areas.
[2] Includes data from Statistics Canada. Population for 1990 reflects data from the 1991 Canadian Census and 2007 reflect data from the 2006 Canadian Census.
Source: U. S. Census Bureau, 2008

enced by the canal cities, and often have smaller cities of their own, such as Binghamton, Elmira, Jamestown, and Watertown. Between these cities is the rural landscape of farms and tiny villages that we often imagine to be upstate but recognize that largely this is not the case.

Table 2.1 shows population figures for 1990 and 2007 for the five largest urban regions that impact the state economy, including figures for areas that are not technically in New York. The definitions are based on the latest (2007 census) definitions of metropolitan areas, but as noted above we have them arranged in a different way.

## New York, New York

We don't want to overstate this, because not everybody or every place in the metropolitan area thrives, but as a place for opportunity, there is still nowhere better than New York City and its suburbs. The 1990s were not necessarily the best for the New York Metropolitan Area, but they were good. The region as a whole grew 11.4 percent, and the city alone grew by 13 percent during the same period. Over 950 thousand people have moved to New York City since 1990, and over 250 thousand since 9/11! The city reached its highest population ever in 2007—8,274,527—and is still growing! And the metropolitan area as a whole grew and the suburbs also did well with a growth rate of over 11 percent. This is not the record of a city or metropolitan area that is in serious economic straits, as New York is only one of two large cities in the northeast to actually gain population. (The other is Boston, so the rivalry continues). It's not uncommon for metropolitan areas to gain population, but it is almost unheard of for northeastern *cities* to grow—growth seems to be primarily a suburban phenomenon. But in New York, the city is actually growing faster than the suburbs, and this is completely anomalous for northeastern metropolitan areas.

Of course, all this growth is not distributed equally in the city. In some cases, neighborhoods like Harlem, for instance, have witnessed a renaissance of upwardly mobile yuppies seeking out the historical significance of one of the most important majority African American neighborhoods in the country (Taylor, 2002). In other inner city neighborhoods, however—such as large areas of upper Manhattan, Brooklyn, and the Bronx—there continues to be high levels of unemployment and poverty as developers tend to look to other areas for investment opportunities. Similarly, looking at a map of growth rates in the metropolitan area shows relative stability in inner suburbs and a rapidly urbanizing urban fringe. The over 12 percent growth in Dutchess and Orange Counties is based primarily on growth in the southern portions of those counties, and is not centered around the central cities of Poughkeepsie, Middletown, and Newburgh. Even the ten percent growth rate for the Kingston Metropolitan Area, ninety miles up the Thruway from New York, is a side effect of downstate suburban growth. As so many folks on Long Island can attest, you can live in the outer suburbs if all you need to do is commute to the inner suburbs. Interestingly, Long Island only grew by 5.8 percent between 1990 and 2007.

Now here's the bad news: that relatively healthy growth rate for Greater New York is still below the national growth rate of 21.3 percent between 1990 and 2007.

## Buffalo Blues

One hundred years ago Buffalo was known throughout the world as one of the greatest cities in the United States. With its stunning architecture and Frederick Law Olmstead-designed park system, Buffalo had a world class infrastructure to match its status. Of course, this infrastructure is still there, but in the mid-twentieth century Buffalo stopped growing whereas its competition did not. Nevertheless, the status of Buffalo depends on which statistics you choose to examine.

In 1990 the Buffalo Metropolitan Area had a population of 1,189,288, but in 2007 this figure had dropped over five percent to 1,128,183. The larger Census

Statistical Area (CSA), which includes Erie, Niagara, and Cattaraugus Counties, similarly dropped from 1,273,522 in 1990 to 1,208,470 in 2007. Most of this loss was due to population declines in central cities with both Buffalo and Niagara Falls losing over fifteen percent of their residents during this time period. But when people left the cities they did not simply move to the suburbs: their populations are best described as stagnant. Erie County minus the city of Buffalo still lost 3,130 residents, and Niagara County minus Niagara Falls gained only 3,603 new residents, meaning that at best many suburbanites switched counties. When one accounts for the natural growth of an area—the increase in population due to the birth of new residents—the Buffalo area has been losing population for decades.

The statistics for Buffalo are complicated because the region lies across the river from Canada. When one adds the Saint Catherine's-Niagara Metropolitan Area to the Buffalo CSA, the region had 1,638,074 in 1990, compared to 1,598,787 in 2007, a loss of only 2.4 percent. This is because growth on the Canadian side of the river between 1991 and 2006 (the years of the Canadian censuses) was over 7 percent. However, the western end of Lake Ontario is Canada's largest megalopolis, stretching from the American border around the end of the lake to Toronto and Oshawa on the lake's northern coast—this area is known as the Golden Horseshoe. Adding just the metropolitan areas hugging the lake shore—Saint-Catherine's-Niagara, Hamilton, Toronto, and Oshawa—yields a population of 6,526,971 in 2007, up 27.9 percent from 5,103,349 in 1990. When metropolitan Buffalo is added to the region, the population in 2007 was 7,735,441 and is projected by Statistics Canada to hit over 11 million by 2030. Buffalo is thus an international city and part of one of the largest urban regions in North America.

Nevertheless, if the trends in Buffalo are so different from those of Toronto, why lump them together? It's simple: Buffalo still has access to that population across the river, and there is considerable demographic and economic integration stretching around the western end of Lake Ontario. The fact that the south shore of the lake, on both sides of the border, grows more slowly than the north shore points to some degree of shared circumstances between Buffalo and her immediate Canadian neighbors, but the sizable population base found at the western end of the lake also points to potential opportunity.

## Rochester

Until recently, Rochester could be called the healthiest metropolitan area in upstate New York, specifically in the city's suburbs. Batavia and Seneca Falls, categorized with Rochester by the Census Bureau, had stable populations, whereas the 3.2 percent growth rate during the 1990s was the result of strength in the

Rochester suburbs. Growth in the last four decades has been driven by such major corporations as Kodak, Bausch & Lomb, Xerox, and a number of smaller firms. This has meant that Rochester has been well connected to the main currents of the global economy. In addition, major research universities contributed to the intellectual and entrepreneurial climate of the region. But there have been major job losses in Rochester since 1990 and it has finally caught up to the region.

On paper, the statistics look good. The Rochester CSA had 1,122,845 in 2007, up 2.46 percent from 1,095,882 in 1990. Buried in these numbers, however, is another picture. Monroe County, the county which contains Rochester, grew from 713,698 residents in 1990 to 735,340 in 2000, but has since dropped to 729,681 in 2007. Suburban Wayne County did the same, growing from 89,123 in 1990 to 93,765 in 2000 before dropping to 91,291 in 2007. In suburban Ontario County, population actually continued to grow from 95,100 in 1990 to 100,224 in 2000 to 103,956 in 2007, but the growth has not been enough to counter a general pattern of population decline since 2000. The other four counties have been generally stable. Nevertheless, much of this population decline was, like Buffalo, centered on Rochester itself as the city lost 10 percent of its population between 1990 and 2000.

## The Capital District

You can hear the snickers already: the Capital District is growing. "Yeah, well, it's because Albany gets all my money." Well, don't go too ballistic, because it's only a 4.7 percent increase for the Albany-Schenectady-Amsterdam CSA between 1990 and 2007, and that is still well below the same figures for the New York Metropolitan Area. In fact, upstate's healthiest large metropolitan area has a growth rate well under half that for New York.

Actually, when you break down the places within this urban region that are growing the fastest, the Glens Falls Metropolitan area (Warren and Washington Counties) is the big winner with an 8.7 percent increase since 1990. The Albany-Schenectady-Troy Metropolitan area only grew by 5.4 percent during the same period, a rather anemic growth rate that is easily explained simply by the natural increase of the area. Saratoga County, just south of Glens Falls and north of Albany, grew the most of any county in the region with a 19 percent growth rate, growing from 181,276 in 1990 to 215,852 in 2007.

Counter balancing this growth in the Hudson Valley is the stagnation of the Mohawk Valley. Both Schenectady and Fulton Counties were roughly stable in population, whereas Montgomery County lost over six percent of its population during this time period.

As with the other upstate metropolitan areas, the central cities are responsible for much of the loss. In the Capital District, however, suburban growth more than makes up for urban population declines. For instance, as the city of Albany lost 7,119 residents between 1990 and 2006, the remainder of Albany County gained 13,832 residents during the same period. In Schenectady County, the city of Schenectady lost 4,006 residents while the remainder of the county gained 5,539; in Rensselaer, Troy lost 6,317 while the remainder of the county gained 7,206. The exception to this rule of suburban growth and center city decline is in Saratoga County, where the city of Saratoga Springs grew 14 percent from 25,001 in 1990 to 28,449 in 2006.

## Central New York

In a region where the two main cities are only 40 miles apart, you can sit in the downtown of one city and listen to a radio station from the other. Several large towns—Oswego, Auburn, Oneida, and Rome—are interspersed with wider areas of open countryside, farmland, and suburban sprawl. In this region of over one million residents, where the Syracuse and Utica skylines grow earth tone towers from the former shores of the Erie Canal, the tallest building in the region was recently completed in... Verona.

Turning Stone Casino, the new pride of the Oneida Indian Nation, is a sprawling and growing resort with several golf courses, a casino, entertainment, and the tallest hotel in central New York. Located in Verona, about twenty miles from both cities, Turning Stone is a glistening tower set amid green golf courses and the sprawling housing developments that line the area around Oneida, Canastota, and Sherrill. Central New York, like Buffalo, has been having problems. The region lost over 38,589 residents since 1990, a loss of 3.6 percent, with the Utica area suffering the biggest loss. In contrast, Flint, Michigan, made famous in Michael Moore's classic documentary *Roger & Me*, grew by one percent during the same time period.

The big culprit appears to have been in manufacturing, particularly that related to defense spending, and the loss of Griffiss Air Force Base in Rome during the 1990s. Contrary to popular opinion, defense spending did not so much decline during the 1990s as shift from the Northeast to the South and West. Some of this was due to corporate mergers that resulted in the scaling back or closure of operations in New York. This is most evident in the city of Rome, which lost 10,130 residents between 1990 and 2006—23 percent of its former population!

**Table 2.2:** Smaller Metropolitan Areas in New York State and Population Change, 1990-2007

| Metropolitan Area | 1990 Population | 2007 Population | Change (%) |
|---|---|---|---|
| Binghamton | 264,497 | 246,426 | -18,071 (-7.6) |
| Elmira | 95,195 | 88,015 | -7,180 (-7.5) |
| Ithaca | 94,097 | 101,055 | 6,958 (7.4) |

Source: U. S. Census Bureau, 2008

## Other Cities

There are, of course, a number of smaller metropolitan areas in the state as well. They are shown in Table 2.2.

Of the remaining three metropolitan areas, only Ithaca has grown since 1990 and it is in fact upstate's fastest growing metropolitan area. Ithaca, as noted earlier, is home to Cornell University, an Ivy League research university that attracts millions of dollars in federal and state research grants every year. Cornell has been particularly involved in its home city, helping to build a new office building downtown and by generally being a fairly good neighbor. Even with this help, however, the metropolitan area only grew by 7.4 percent, slightly over half the growth rate for New York City.

Binghamton is the largest city of the southern tier and home to Binghamton University—one of the four major university centers of the State University of New York (SUNY). Binghamton has lost over seven percent of its population since 1990; like central New York the population decline was largely in response to the movement of defense spending from the northeast to other regions of the country. About an hour to the west is Elmira, which has similarly faced a slide in population. This pattern is part of a general malaise that set over the Southern Tier of New York State.

## Micropolitan & Rural Areas

Population trends in the state's micropolitan areas—large towns that perform many of the same functions as metropolitan areas in their respective regions but without the population to qualify them as "metropolitan areas"—are shown in Figure 2.3. Upon inspection one notices that the average micropolitan area appears to have lost population, but with only a—0.7 percent decline it is safer to say that micropolitan areas have experienced relative stability. Unfortunately, population stability is not a good sign. In the United States, birth rates tend to outpace death rates, so we should expect most areas—if not specific communities—to at least gain some population as more people are born than

**Table 2.3:** Micropolitan Areas in New York State and Population Change, 1990-2007

| Micropolitan Area | 1990 Population | 2007 Population | Change (%) |
|---|---|---|---|
| Corning | 99,088 | 96874 | -2,214 (-2.2) |
| Cortland | 48,963 | 48369 | -594 (-1.2) |
| Jamestown-Dunkirk-Fredonia | 141,895 | 133945 | -7,950 (-5.6) |
| Malone | 46,540 | 50449 | 3,909 (8.4) |
| Ogdensburg-Massena | 111,974 | 109809 | -2,165 (-1.9) |
| Oneonta | 60,517 | 62397 | 1,880 (3.11) |
| Plattsburgh | 85,969 | 82215 | -3,754 (-4.37) |
| Watertown | 110,943 | 117201 | 6,258 (5.64) |
| **TOTAL** | **705,899** | **701,259** | **-4,630 (-0.7)** |

Source: U. S. Census Bureau, 2008

die. Population stability is thus an indication that the excess population created by the higher birth rate is leaving the community. Or put more simply, many micropolitan areas are able to maintain their own local economies, but they also face a constant outflow of youth to other places.

Table 2.4 shows population trends for the eleven New York counties that are not classified as either metropolitan or micropolitan; that is, the counties classified as rural. On average, rural counties grew by 2.5 percent. Based on that figure, we might conclude that rural New York is in good shape. Until, of course, we look a bit closer.

Only three of the eleven rural counties have growth rates that mimic those found in the New York Metropolitan area. Two of these—Greene and Sullivan—are counties immediately adjacent to the New York metropolitan area, and they account for nearly two-thirds of the population growth in rural New York counties during the 1990s. The third county with such a high growth rate is Yates County in the Finger Lakes, immediately adjacent to the Rochester metropolitan area. Yates appears to have the highest growth rate, but with a 1990 pop-

**Table 2.4:** Rural Counties in New York State and Population Change, 1990-2007

| County | 1990 Population | 2007 Population | Change (%) |
|---|---|---|---|
| Allegany | 50,970 | 49,367 | -1,603 (-3.1) |
| Chenango | 51,768 | 51,207 | -561 (-1.1) |
| Delaware | 47,352 | 46,286 | -1,066 (-2.3) |
| Essex | 37,152 | 38,119 | 967 (2.6) |
| Greene | 44,739 | 49,246 | 4,507 (10.1) |
| Hamilton | 5,279 | 5,075 | -204 (-2.9) |
| Lewis | 26,796 | 26,472 | -324 (-1.1) |
| Schuyler | 18,662 | 19,027 | 365 (2.0) |
| Sullivan | 69,277 | 76,303 | 7,026 (10.1) |
| Wyoming | 42,507 | 41,932 | -575 (-1.4) |
| Yates | 22,810 | 24,557 | 1,747 (7.7) |
| **TOTAL** | **417,312** | **417,312** | **10,279 (2.5)** |

Source: U. S. Census Bureau, 2008

ulation of less than 23 thousand residents, its 7.9 percent increase amounts to less than 2,000 new residents. Similarly, Essex County, in the Adirondacks with the Northway running from end to end, gained 1,699 residents during the 1990s—a 4.6 percent increase. Take these counties out of the table, and a picture remarkably similar to that of the micropolitan areas is evident: population stability. Which is, of course, another way of saying stagnation.

## Another Look at the Issue

If the various metropolitan areas and rural communities show a certain diversity within the state, one still notices certain constraints based on regional characteristics that extend beyond the state's borders. What we often think of as the upstate/downstate divide in actuality extends into New England and down the spine of the Appalachians. New York sits astride one of America's cultural and economic dividing lines. The growth in the New York metropolitan area is part of a larger pattern of growth that extends along the Eastern seaboard. If one examines the ten fastest growing metropolitan areas in the northeast as a whole, one notices an interesting trait: all but two are part of the northeast corridor megalopolis (see Table 2.5).

All of the metropolitan areas have populations of below one million people, except for New York, of course. Boston and Philadelphia—eleventh and twelfth, respectively—fill out this list of coastal metropolitan areas. Does this mean that smaller cities are favored in the northeast? No! Except for two—the same two not part of the northeast megalopolis—they are all within an hour drive of the large metropolitan areas of New York, Philadelphia, Boston, and Washington-

**Table 2.5:** The Ten Fastest Growing Northeastern Metropolitan Areas, 1990-2000

| MSA (CMSA) | Unemployment Rate | 1990 Population | 2000 Population | Percent Change |
|---|---|---|---|---|
| Barnstable-Yarmouth, MA | 4.4 | 134,954 | 162,582 | 20.47 |
| York, PA | 3.6 | 339,574 | 381,751 | 12.42 |
| Burlington, VT | 3.9 | 151,506 | 169,391 | 11.80 |
| Lancaster, PA | 3.0 | 422,822 | 470,658 | 11.31 |
| Reading, PA | 5.1 | 336,523 | 373,638 | 11.03 |
| Portland, ME | 3.6 | 221,095 | 243,537 | 10.15 |
| State College, PA | 5.5 | 123,786 | 135,758 | 9.67 |
| New York, NY | 6.7 | 19,549,649 | 21,199,865 | 8.44 |
| Allenton-Bethlehem, PA | 4.6 | 595,081 | 637,958 | 7.21 |
| Harrisburg-Lebanon-Carlisle, PA | 3.9 | 587,986 | 629,401 | 7.04 |

Source: U. S. Census, 2008

Baltimore. Which inland northeastern metropolitan areas buck the trend of anemic growth? Burlington, Vermont and State College, Pennsylvania. What do these cities have in common? They are both home to major state universities—the University of Vermont and Pennsylvania State University. Does this mean that cities with universities are favored? Consider the statistics in Table 2.6. The table looks only at inland metropolitan areas in the northeast. Although there appear to be major differences, the only statistically significant difference is median family income—metropolitan areas with research universities have higher average incomes. Median Family Income, on the other hand, is positively correlated with population growth ($r=0.634$, $p=.001$) and negatively correlated with unemployment ($r=-0.634$, $p=.001$). Does this mean that the presence of a college determines a city's fate? No. First, notice that the statistics are limited to research universities—institutions like the University of Buffalo/SUNY, Syracuse University, and Rochester Institute of Technology. The positive effects of research universities declines when replaced with other types of institutions, although having even a community college is better than none at all. Second, not even having a research university guarantees success. Syracuse and Binghamton are both home to major universities, and both lost considerable population during the 1990s. If one looks at the three upstate metropolitan areas to gain population during the 1990s, Albany is home to two research universities (University at Albany/SUNY and Rensselaer Polytechnic Institute), Rochester is also home to two (Rochester Institute of Technology and the University of Rochester), and Ithaca is home to one (Cornell University). Because Ithaca has less than 100 thousand residents, over a fifth of its population is connected directly to Cornell University. So, a research university helps a city considerably, but it is not a magic bullet.

So why do universities and colleges help a community's chances? Before we can answer that, we should again digress and look at the ten slowest growing metropolitan areas in the northeast. These are in Table 2.7.

**Table 2.6:** Socioeconomic Characteristics of Inland Metropolitan Areas with and without Research Universities

| | Unemployment Rate | Median Family Income | Poverty Rate | 1990-2000 Population Change |
|---|---|---|---|---|
| Research University MSAs | 5.6 | 50723 | 12.5 | 1.91 |
| Non-Research University MSAs | 5.9 | 44016 | 11.5 | -0.61 |
| Average of All MSAs | 5.8 | 46932 | 11.9 | 0.48 |

[1] $F=0.869, p=.362$

[2] $F=14.427, p=.001$

[3] $F=.943, p=.343$

[4] $F=1.609, p=.219$

Source: U. S. Census, 2008

**Table 2.7:** The Ten Slowest Growing Northeastern Metropolitan Areas, 1990-2000

| MSA (CMSA) | Unemployment Rate | 1990 Population | 2000 Population | Percent Change |
|---|---|---|---|---|
| Utica-Rome, NY | 6.1 | 316,633 | 299,896 | -5.29 |
| Binghamton, NY | 5.3 | 264,497 | 252,300 | -4.61 |
| Pittsfield, MA | 5.5 | 88,695 | 84,699 | -4.51 |
| Elmira, NY | 7.8 | 95,195 | 91,070 | -4.33 |
| Johnstown, PA | 7.7 | 241,247 | 232,621 | -3.58 |
| Lewiston-Auburn, ME | 5.1 | 93,679 | 90,830 | -3.04 |
| Scranton-Wilkes Barre, PA | 5.6 | 638,466 | 624,776 | -2.14 |
| Buffalo-Niagara Falls, NY | 7.0 | 1,189,288 | 1,170,111 | -1.61 |
| Jamestown, NY | 6.3 | 141,895 | 139,750 | -1.51 |
| Pittsburgh, PA | 5.8 | 2,394,811 | 2,358,695 | -1.51 |

Source: U. S. Census, 2008

One immediately notices that they are all at a distance from the northeast megalopolis. Some are quite large, like Buffalo and Pittsburgh. Some are small, like Elmira and Lewiston-Auburn. Some have major universities like Binghamton, some do not. All they have in common is a geographical separation from the large coastal metropolitan areas. Besides differences in growth rates, does being inland make a difference on quality of life? This is shown in Table 2.8. In all cases, coastal metropolitan areas are significantly healthier in terms of employment, income, poverty and, not surprisingly, population growth. Both in the case of geography and the presence of a university, the root condition that generates economic health is the integration of the community with the wider global economy.

The good news for upstate New York is that geography is not fate, and in fact a concerted effort to better integrate upstate communities with the down

**Table 2.8:** Socioeconomic Characteristics of Northeastern Coastal and Inland Metropolitan Areas

| | Unemployment Rate[1] | Median Family Income[2] | Poverty Rate[3] | 1990-2000 Population Change[4] |
|---|---|---|---|---|
| East Coast MSAs | 4.8 | $55,709 | 9.3 | 7.56 |
| Inland MSAs | 5.8 | $46,932 | 11.9 | 0.48 |
| Average of All MSAs | 5.4 | $50,101 | 10.9 | 3.0 |

[1] $F=6.684, p=.014$
[2] $F=24.376, p=.00$
[3] $F=9.545, p=.004$
[4] $F=16.471, p=.00$

Source: U. S. Census, 2008

state economy is the key to changing the fortunes of both upstate and the state as whole. We know that the presence of a university helps to integrate a community by attracting students, highly educated researchers, and entrepreneurs. This mix helps to integrate the community with the wider system, and this integration helps to further attract new talent to the city. But since the presence of a university does not guarantee success, it is not a viable policy option on its own. Other institutions can also serve to integrate communities into the global economy, and we should explore them. For example, the internet can help to better integrate communities. In the end, of course, investment in an electronic infrastructure cannot replace investment in transportation—it can only supplement it. A quick look at the highway system for New York City might lead one to believe that the state policy has been to move people from New York City into New Jersey, and the highways that do lead north seem to have too few lanes and too many drivers.

## Four Myths about New York's Decline

It seems that everybody has their own pet theory for what is happening in New York. In talking to people all over upstate New York, there are many different reasons cited for the demise of upstate. Just as often, however, there is little actual evidence brought to support one's contentions, or the evidence that is offered contradicts other evidence that might be used to refute the claims. While there are so many reasons cited, we found that many of the major reasons break down into four major areas of concern. We refer to them as the four myths about New York's decline.

### *Myth 1: It's the Weather*

Okay, this is a tough one. As I write this in March 2005, we just went through a period of two weeks where it snowed every day. Even the skiers and snowmobilers seem ready for a change! And it is true that the warmest area of the state—downstate—is also the healthiest. But climate is normally a secondary consideration when it comes to migrations. In a modern economy, people tend to follow jobs. That is, if workers perceive a sense of opportunity in a nasty climate, they tend to migrate there. If the next generation still senses the opportunity to have a decent life and fulfill their ambitions in a nasty climate, they stay. Now let's think about upstate New York in this context.

Certainly, as difficult as it is to stay warm today it was more difficult two hundred years ago. However, beginning in the 1790s, migrants from New England—a generally better climate—began to flood the region in search of cheap land. In other words, they came from a comparatively warm climate—at least those coming from Massachusetts, Connecticut, and Rhode Island—to a colder and certainly snowier climate because they perceived that they could have a future here. Indeed, the millions of immigrants who found their way from Mediterranean climates like Italy, Greece, and Spain left their warm climate for the opportunity of the upstate winter. Even Ireland has a better climate! So in terms of settling the region, climate was not a barrier because migrants were looking for economic opportunity.

That was then, this is now? No. For instance, Ohio is also downwind of the Great Lakes, and thus like upstate faces exorbitant levels of snow, yet weathered the 1990s in better shape than upstate New York. Similarly, even the name "Vermont" conjures images of healthy small towns in the pristine wilderness, whereas their neighbors to the west do not. Let's face it: if there is economic opportunity, people most often like to stay near family and friends regardless of the weather. Simply stated, populations that are economically and socially secure learn to ski in the face of winter, they don't move.

### *Myth 2: It's the Workforce*

A friend of mine summed it up: "my parents had lots of trouble finding reliable employees for their business." Okay, let's say that's true. Are people really different in other states? Is there some strange genetic quality in New Yorkers that makes us poor workers? If there is, it somehow developed in the last two-hundred years. Even if good workers are hard to find in New York, that does not mean that they are easier to find somewhere else. In fact, a look at some basic statistics shows that upstate is in many ways a *better* place to find good workers than other places.

A recent Brookings Institute report on the economy of upstate New York examined New York's system of higher education, and found that upstate's 206 higher education institutions results in the region having a higher proportion of college graduates than the nation as a whole—32.8 percent upstate compared to 30.7 percent nationwide (Pendall et al, 2004). There are issues with New York's higher education system that need to be addressed, and we will do so in chapter 6, but you cannot say that New York has a less educated workforce. And an educated workforce tends to be more productive than less educated workforces.

As noted by the recent Brookings Institute reports, education is a strength for upstate New York. Every year, thousands of young people migrate to upstate New York to live for four years, but then many of those who want to go to graduate or professional school must often leave to find a program. The problem is not that there are not enough schools, but rather that upstate New York colleges could be utilized to a much greater extent than they are. Consider this: in the entire region, there are only 4 law schools (Cornell University, Syracuse University, Albany Law School, and SUNY Buffalo), only 2 medical schools (Albany Medical College, Upstate Medical Center), 2 doctoral level technology universities (Rensellaer Polytechnic Institutute, Rochester Institute of Technology), and 6 comprehensive research universities (SUNY Buffalo, SUNY Binghamton, SUNY Albany, University of Rochester, Syracuse University, and Cornell University). These schools help their respective cities considerably, and one would think that we should build on such strengths in order to stay ahead of other regions in one of the few areas where upstate really is ahead.

Realistically, do you honestly think people in upstate New York are dumber or slower than people in Texas, North Carolina or California? We wouldn't claim that New Yorkers are, as a group, smarter or faster than folks in other states, but we likewise wouldn't claim inferiority either. Blaming the workforce is a quick and easy way of justifying why you might leave a community once you have made the decision, but if the grass is greener somewhere else it is only because you don't see the divots and the dry spots from a distance. It's not the workforce; indeed, upstate New York compares quite favorably.

### *Myth 3: Free Trade is killing us*

As will be evident from chapter 5, free trade has not been entirely positive for New York. In fact, there are a number of common-sense reforms to our federal trade policies that would help New York immensely, and had they been implemented initially perhaps we would not have declined to the degree that we have. That said, free trade is not a lone gunmen, nor even the most deadly, and we should acknowledge that.

A drive through Utica shows one of the greatest areas of decline in upstate's economy: textiles. Utica and its suburbs was once a major producer of textiles, home to two of the largest textile companies in the world in 1920 and producer of world famous brands like Duofold underwear, Oneita shirts, and Utica sheets. Those companies didn't move overseas, but rather to the south, where workers would work for less pay and the equipment in the new factories was, well, new. Even had these companies stayed in the region, modernizing their plants would likely have cost thousands of jobs as well. Much the same can be said of older production lines for other items once made in New York as well: people would still have lost jobs to robots, and some companies would have gone under in the face of new competition.

In fact, many of the jobs lost since World War II were not lost to New York companies moving factories overseas, but rather were lost to New York companies being taken over by out-of-state firms who subsequently shut down New York facilities in favor of plants in other states. One recent example is General Electric Aerospace, a defense contractor in Syracuse and Utica. During the

1990s, the division was sold first to Martin Marietta Corporation, who maintained the factories. Within a few years, however, Martin Marietta merged with Lockheed Corporation to become Lockheed Martin. Lockheed Martin already had factories that performed many of the same functions as the New York plants, and subsequently closed or downsized their upstate operations. These job losses were not due solely to any free trade agreements, but rather to corporate mergers.

### *Myth 4: Taxes!*

We saved the big one for last, and we'll discuss it the longest. Everyone, both Democrats and Republicans, in New York seems to know that taxes are the main reason for the decline. Well, let's look at state taxes first. In Table 2.9, we see the ten states with the highest state tax burdens, and there is New York in the number 9 slot. One curious fact is that New York's growth rate of 1.7 percent between 2000 and 2006 is lower than those for the eight states with higher state taxes; in fact, the only state on the top ten to have a slower rate is Massachusetts, and their taxes are slightly lower. But the key figure is perhaps not state taxes, but state and local taxes combined. When state taxes are combined with all those local taxes—county, town, city, school district, water district, lighting district, special use districts, etc.—New York begins to look much worse. On average, local taxes nearly double the tax burden on New Yorkers.

In contrast, in Table 2.10, we compare New York to the ten states with the lowest state tax burden per capita. At first glance it appears that the low tax states have faster growth rates, but this observation does not hold across the board. A number of low tax states have rates that do not exceed the high tax states, such as Alabama, South Dakota, and even Missouri. More ominously, one also notices that, with the exception of New Hampshire, Florida and Colorado, the low tax states all have poverty rates over 12 percent. Among the high tax states, only New York has that distinction, and most states are below 10 percent. On average, the high tax states received almost as much spending from the federal government as they paid in taxes, but on closer examination that includes Alaska and Hawaii, two states that have rather special spending requirements due to their locations. Exclude these two states, and the remaining high tax states only receive 82 cents for every dollar they pay in federal taxes. Only Wyoming makes a profit. In comparison, the low tax states received an average of $1.14 in federal spending for every dollar they paid in.

**Table 2.9:** The Ten Highest State Tax Burdens

| State | Population, 2006 | Population Change, 2000-2006 (%) | Per Capita State Tax, 2007 ($) | Per Capita State & Local Tax, 2006 ($) | Median Household Income, 2004 | Poverty Rate, 2004 | Federal Spending, 2004 ($1000) | Federal Spending per Capita, 2004 |
|---|---|---|---|---|---|---|---|---|
| Alaska | 670.053 | 6.9 | 5,037 | 5,410 | 52,141 | 10.0 | 8,445,389 | 1.84 |
| Vermont | 623,908 | 2.5 | 4,119 | 4,435 | 44,548 | 8.7 | 4,632,933 | 1.08 |
| Hawaii | 1,285,537 | 6.1 | 3,969 | 4,848 | 51,359 | 9.0 | 12,187,069 | 1.44 |
| Wyoming | 515,004 | 4.3 | 3,873 | 6,116 | 43,785 | 10.3 | 4,393,308 | 1.11 |
| Connecticut | 3,504,809 | 2.9 | 3,668 | 5,685 | 56,617 | 9.1 | 30,303,984 | 0.69 |
| Minnesota | 5,167,101 | 5.0 | 3,421 | 4,363 | 51,202 | 8.1 | 28,790,741 | 0.72 |
| Delaware | 853,476 | 8.9 | 3,360 | 4,243 | 49,545 | 9.6 | 5,253,147 | 0.77 |
| New Jersey | 8,724,560 | 3.7 | 3,351 | 5,459 | 57,338 | 8.4 | 55,264,350 | 0.61 |
| New York | 19,306,183 | 1.7 | 3,273 | 6,413 | 45,343 | 14.5 | 143,902,576 | 0.79 |
| Massachusetts | 6,437,193 | 1.4 | 3,204 | 4,761 | 53,657 | 9.9 | 53,120,445 | 0.82 |
| **Average of Ten Highest States** | **4,708,782** | **4.34** | **3,728** | **5,173.30** | **50,553.50** | **9.76** | **34,329,394** | **0.99** |

Source: US Census, 2008; Tax Foundation; Federation of Tax Administrators

**Table 2.10:** The Ten Lowest State Tax Burdens

| State | Population | Population Change, 2000-2006 (%) | Per Capita State Tax, 2007 ($) | Per Capita State & Local Tax, 2006 ($) | Median Household Income, 2004 | Poverty Rate, 2004 | Federal Spending, 2004 | Federal Spending per Dollar of Federal Tax, 2005 |
|---|---|---|---|---|---|---|---|---|
| Florida | 18,089,888 | 13.2 | 1,958 | 3,693 | 40,900 | 11.9 | 121,933,502 | 0.97 |
| Arizona | 6,166,318 | 20.2 | 1,956 | 3,234 | 43,696 | 14.6 | 41,979,303 | 1.19 |
| Georgia | 9,363,941 | 14.4 | 1,953 | 3,321 | 42,679 | 13.7 | 55,152,911 | 1.01 |
| Alabama | 4,599,030 | 3.4 | 1,916 | 2,782 | 37,062 | 16.1 | 39,047,473 | 1.66 |
| Colorado | 4,753,377 | 10.5 | 1,894 | 3,614 | 50,105 | 10.2 | 30,060,329 | 0.81 |
| Tennessee | 6,038,803 | 6.1 | 1,843 | 2,838 | 38,945 | 15.0 | 45,440,543 | 1.27 |
| Missouri | 5,842,713 | 4.4 | 1,821 | 3,137 | 40,885 | 13.0 | 45,730,137 | 1.32 |
| Texas | 23,507,783 | 12.7 | 1,686 | 3,235 | 41,645 | 16.2 | 141,858,480 | 0.94 |
| New Hampshire | 1,314,895 | 6.4 | 1,651 | 3,443 | 53,377 | 6.6 | 7,958,518 | 0.71 |
| South Dakota | 781,919 | 3.6 | 1,578 | 2,842 | 39,265 | 12.9 | 6,601,736 | 1.53 |
| *New York* | *19,306,183* | *1.7* | *3,273* | *6,413* | *45,343* | *14.5* | *143,902,576* | *0.79* |
| **Average of Ten Highest States** | **8,045,866** | **9.49** | **1,826** | **3,214** | **42,856** | **13.0** | **53,576,293** | **1.14** |

Source: US Census, 2008; Tax Foundation; Federation of Tax Administrators

The picture that we receive from looking at this data is that taxes are an important contributor to a region's well being, but they alone do not determine a region's fortunes. Note from the various passages in this chapter that downstate is economically healthier than upstate, with the metropolitan area experiencing a healthy population growth rate and the city itself gaining enough new residents during the 1990s to have the highest recorded population in its history. And, they pay higher taxes than upstate residents: in local income taxes—unheard of upstate—and higher property taxes, as well as tolls and mass transit. Metropolitan New York is simply a more expensive area in which to live. So much so that the statistics for the state as a whole are skewed upward, and the statistics for the state as a whole include downstate's high tax burden; and still it is booming. It's the comparatively low tax, low wage, no local income tax region of the state—places like Buffalo and central New York and the multiple little towns with shuttered storefronts—that are suffering.

Yes, New York City has large swaths of poverty and we do not mean to minimize that; indeed, the City has a higher poverty rate than that found in most upstate counties. But that is not a fair comparison, as measuring poverty in New York City does not, by definition, include the sprawling and generally healthy suburbs. And in a city of eight million people, huge areas of poverty are to be expected, although they should not necessarily be acceptable. However, as a region, the New York Metropolitan Area is healthier than any area upstate, except those in the frontline of New York's ever expanding suburbs. If the highest tax region of the state is healthier than the lowest taxed area, this at the very least says that we cannot look to taxes alone as the culprit in New York's problems.

## Contributing Factors

We need to look at all of the myths as contributing factors even if we cannot scapegoat them entirely. The weather in upstate New York is not the type of weather that most people dream of. Yes, we have four seasons, but that fourth one could use some shortening. Some people are going to move because of the weather. But that does not mean that upstate needs to flounder: some people don't mind the weather, and a good job or a nice place to live in other respects will be enough to keep them here. New York has a workforce that is, on average, more highly educated than most places, but that does not mean that there are no ways to improve education and workforce development. Free Trade agreements have, overall, not been helpful to New York's economy, but there are other factors that we need to look at as well. Certainly, we might not want to keep expanding "free trade," but we don't want to scapegoat it either. And finally, although "high taxes" is overblown as a reason for upstate's demise, we cannot say that there is no room for improvement. Simply stated, there is room for improvement and we need to find ways to streamline our tax and local governance system. That said, we shouldn't look at high taxes as a primary cause for stagnation or decline, and we shouldn't look at low taxes as a panacea for the problem.

One thing is for sure: if we, as New Yorkers, allow such a split between a prosperous downstate and a depressed upstate to continue, we will regret the ramifications. Picture a New York Metropolitan Area forced, by political fact, to give more and more of its income to suffering upstate counties. Picture the politicians who will emerge from upstate willing to exploit such inequality, savagely scapegoating New Yorkers for even the smallest infractions in their small towns. Or, conversely, think of the changes that will take place if every moderately wealthy New Yorker takes advantage of lower real estate prices upstate to have their own vacation home. How will the locals afford a house of their own? In short, how sustainable do you think this inequality will be in the long run?

A quick read of this chapter makes apparent that New York 1) needs to reform its system of government, and 2) needs to make investments that will better integrate the entire state in the future. If we consider the four major parameters of a society we discussed in the introduction—polity, economy, culture, and environment—we can see that while the four myths discussed above do seem to hit on the issues, they also tend to oversimplify our problems. Let's think about New York's issues in reverse order. Consider the climate, for instance. While this is an environmental factor, so is the built environment of the state, i.e. the infrastructure. This includes our railroads, airports, highways, cell towers and the internet. What can be done to improve the natural and built environment of the state? Or consider cultural concerns: have New Yorkers really considered all the options, or are we accepting the idea that New York faces stiff competition from the Sun Belt and overseas, and thus there is nothing we can do? Often, our notion of the economy is simplified to our high taxes, but these are only part of the problem. And finally, do the political powers that be in New York think "outside the box" or do we see ideas developed within a particular mindset? And do our leaders even recognize that there is a particular mindset?

These are not new issues in New York policy circles, and it may help to examine a policy that was controversial at the time but proved to be a tremendous success: the building of the Erie Canal. In the next chapter, we will consider the canal as a policy that had, and continues to have, a major impact on the future development of New York State.

# Empire State Building 3

There is perhaps no more important policy decision made in the history of New York State than whether or not to build the Erie Canal. Begun in Rome in 1817, the canal was actually the latest in a series of proposals for canals linking the east coast to the Great Lakes. A French engineer proposed a canal linking Lakes Erie and Ontario in 1699, but it was Cadwallader Colden who first suggested a link from the Hudson to Lake Erie in 1724. A series of letters and reports suggested numerous other proposals as well, including the construction of locks around major falls at Canajoharie and Little Falls or building only to Lake Ontario. In 1786 a bill to improve navigation along the Mohawk River, Woods Creek and the Onondaga River to Oswego went down to defeat in the legislature, but six years later the *Western Inland Lock Navigation Company* was formed to do roughly the same thing. It succeeded in building the first navigation locks in the United States at Little Falls, but ultimately failed in its endeavor to improve navigation. After much political wrangling, a law authorizing the building of the Erie Canal was passed on April 17, 1816. Construction began on the Fourth of July the following year at Rome, proceeding east and west along the relatively flat landscape to Utica and Syracuse so that good progress could be shown early in the process.

The canal would work because of the unique environment of its route: the canal and the Hudson River form the only natural and navigable pass through the Appalachian Upland from Maine to Georgia—even better than the famed Cumberland Gap! It's construction relied on the economic investment on the part of the state, and such a large investment (over $7.1 million) was unheard of at the time. Needless to say, it took considerable political will to make such an investment; this will required considerable imagination on the part of New York's leaders to see not what the canal region was at the time—primarily a collection of rural villages connected by a few toll roads such as the Western Turnpike and the Genesee Highway—but what the region could become.

## Growing the Empire

In 1825, Governor DeWitt Clinton witnessed the fulfillment of a dream. In that year he had the privilege of dumping a bucket of water collected in Lake Erie in Buffalo into New York Harbor (Cornog, 2000). It had been transported to New York City by way of the newly built Erie Canal, and the ceremony thus symbolized the merging of the waters. To say that the Erie Canal is responsible for the greatness of the Empire State would not be an exaggeration. Even today, the vast majority of the state's residents live within twenty miles of this thin ribbon of water. It was the main corridor to the Great Lakes and the spur to development from Albany to Buffalo. And it almost was not built.

Throughout the 1810s, deriders of the canal slandered it as "Clinton's Ditch," suggesting that a fiscally responsible approach to state finances would not build such an obvious boondoggle. A canal from the Hudson to the Great Lakes was viewed as little more than a giant pork project that would benefit only New York City merchants and a handful of residents along the path. Besides, there had been similar projects that failed. A canal in Little Falls attempted to bypass the rapids in the Mohawk River at that point, and was a failure—both financially and technologically. Even after the Erie Canal was started in 1817, canal supporters were careful to pick a location where the canal could be an almost instant success. They began in Rome and dug a four foot deep ditch to Utica only fifteen miles away, through the relatively flat and fertile Mohawk Valley where it flows from the Great Lakes plain. Naturally, work progressed quickly, as did similar work from Rome toward Syracuse (which was not yet Syracuse) along the Lake Ontario plain itself. The early success of the canal helped to quiet naysayers and kept the project going for the next seven years, even as work got bogged down in Montezuma Swamp and technological difficulties presented themselves in the great series of locks at Lockport and Cohoes (Larkin, 1998). Yes, 1825 was a great year for DeWitt Clinton, and opened a new age in New York.

Prior to the building of the canal, immigration into upstate New York came primarily in the form of farmers from New England. As farmland became more expensive in the early 1800s, many farmers and potential immigrants simply looked even further west in the frontier of the Ohio Country and beyond. For many eastern counties, the great Yankee migration appeared over. For instance, in Otsego County, south of the Mohawk River at the headwaters of the Susquehanna, the rather rocky hillsides filled up quickly between 1790 and 1810, but by 1820 the county's population had peaked at about 50 thousand residents. Otsego County remained at roughly that population throughout the rest of the nineteenth century and even into the twentieth, even as the small city of Oneonta grew at its southern border at the turn of the century. In fact, the rapid growth of Oneonta between 1890 and 1910 only made up for population that was lost from the rural towns during the same time period. The reality was that rural Otsego County lost considerable population during the nineteenth century, whereas Oneonta gained enough new residents to make it look like Otsego County remained at the same population throughout the period (Thomas, 2005).

Otsego is a microcosm of the pattern found in upstate counties at a distance from the Erie Canal. For instance, Schoharie County lost nearly a third of its population throughout the late nineteenth and early twentieth centuries as former farm children abandoned the lifestyle of their parents and moved to the cities. The exception to Schoharie County's population slide was the village of Cobleskill, which at about 3,000 residents was the county's largest population center. A similar pattern was evident in Delaware County, where villages like Sidney and Walton grew even as the farming areas lost considerable population. So at a time when much of New York State was growing very rapidly, what was happening in rural New York?

The answer is not to be found in the rural villages themselves, but rather in larger societal forces that were hard to comprehend at the moment but more apparent in hindsight. Part of the problem was a cultural and economic shift in the way farming was practiced. Yes, technology played a role, in particular in the early twentieth century, but many communities witnessed a change after 1840—before technology had such a marked impact. What had changed was a shift from subsistence agriculture to one oriented toward Capitalism and trade with the growing cities. Whereas the earliest settlers were in search of a somewhat independent existence, by the mid-nineteenth century they were increasingly growing crops not for their own use but for the markets of the growing cities. This meant that farmers increasingly participated in the urban economy—dominated as it was by money as a medium of exchange—rather than the small local economies driven as much or more by a system in which farmers helped one another in the fields and grew primarily in order to keep themselves and their families alive. In other words, farming switched from subsistence agriculture to a market driven agriculture, and this changed the way a household would be arranged. In the past a farm household would often include an extended family and a number of farm workers, and this benefited the larger household as more people meant more work could be done. But with a market driven agricultural economy, farmers increasingly needed to keep overhead low in order to make a higher profit from the crops—too many farm workers were now a drain on the bottom line. And so, as this new economy took root, many farm laborers and even family members were forced off the farms and to places where non-farm employment could be found. And this normally meant the larger villages in a region and, increasingly, the rapidly growing cities.

There were other reasons for population decline in rural areas as well. Increasingly throughout the nineteenth century, popular magazines and newspapers praised the latest technological accomplishments, and these were normally urban accomplishments. Just as today, many youth dreamed of working with technological marvels and taking advantage of the opportunities to be found in the cities. And so, as the nineteenth century wore on, many farming communities were slowly depopulated of their youth—especially those bright and ambitious enough to chance a move to the big city. And New York had those high technology centers in abundance: the wonders of steam power in Utica and Buffalo in mid-century; electricity in Niagara Falls and Schenectady due to such people as George Westinghouse, Nikola Tesla, and Thomas Edison in the late nineteenth century; and photography in Rochester after George Eastman invented film in 1884. And of course, the great skyscrapers of Manhattan inspired as much awe then as today. The cities of New York offered an array of high technology wonders that attracted not only rural New Yorkers off the farm but pulled people from other states and nations as well. But they were not simply attracted to the state, but to particular points within the state. And these points were most often in the corridor of the Hudson River and Erie Canal.

## The Great Corridor

The great corridor created by the building of the Erie Canal was not simply a "canal corridor." What the canal did more than anything else was establish a corridor where transportation would be quite inexpensive, and in doing so it selected which communities could thrive through the transportation industry and which would not. For instance, the canal spurred much growth in the salt flats near Onondaga Lake. The salt could be transported cheaply to New York on the coast or to Buffalo and beyond in the Great Lakes region. The burgeoning industry lead to rapid population increases as workers in the industry itself as well as those merchants and land speculators willing to make money off the explosion flooded to the various townships around the canal. By mid-century, three towns merged and became known as Syracuse. The growth continued as the initial population surge led to new entrepreneurs and new industries; and thus even more people. Similarly, at the point where the Erie Canal crossed the rambunctious Genesee River, the village of Rochester grew rapidly throughout the nineteenth century, spawning new industries and attracting entrepreneurs and inventors. The city gave birth to Kodak and Bausch & Lomb. These dynamics were set in motion by the arrival of the Erie Canal, and even early on any new technology or transportation route of necessity would include these cities. And so, as railroads were built shortly after the Erie Canal in the 1830s and 1840s, the Erie Canal corridor cities of Schenectady, Utica, Syracuse, Rochester, and Buffalo were important transportation centers that a potential railroad tycoon neglected at great risk. The individual Railroad companies built during this period, such as the Schenectady & Utica, the Utica & Syracuse—you get the idea—eventually were incorporated as the New York Central & Hudson River Railroad, running from New York to Buffalo and eventually to Chicago. The railroads competed against the canal, giving freight transporters and passengers new options. Ship it yourself by horse and wagon, ship it by canal packet boat, or ship it by rail. Each had its own advantages. Do it yourself and cut out the middleman, but it will take a long time. Ship it by canal and stay home, but it will still take a while. Ship it by rail and get it there faster, but expect to pay more. Don't like the New York Central—ship it on the West Shore Railroad. Or, by the end of the century, by one of the various electric "interurban" trolleys. The upstate trolley system ran from the eastern suburbs of Utica to the western suburbs of Rochester! In other words, the importance of the canal corridor itself was not necessarily the canal itself, but rather the multitude of competing transportation technologies available to the entrepreneur. This multitude of options in the great corridor made it a great place for manufacturing, but ultimately did little for counties outside the corridor.

In the social sciences, this observation is referred to as combined and uneven development. Economic development is combined in areas that have access to the larger economic system—then the national economy increasingly dominated by New York City traders and today the global economy. Access to this system in the form of transportation meant that a community had expanding markets and the benefits of technology and infrastructure flowing from the larger system. Upstate communities received capital and resources from New York investors and inventers, with places like Schenectady benefiting from the inventions of people like Thomas Edison. Downstate received relatively cheap goods to trade on the international market from upstate, like Kodak cameras, Carrier air conditioners, Remington typewriters, and Westinghouse generators, to say nothing of the investment opportunities that such firms represented. Away from this system, however, development was uneven—it tended to lag behind the cities, and was often utilized as a source of food, raw materials, or even tourism, but not as an area that received a substantial amount of capital investment. Indeed, at times the tutelage of the upper classes in the form of tourism translates into a desire on their part to keep the community the same, and so their presence does not translate into economic development.

For instance, Table 3.1 shows the fastest and slowest growing counties between 1850 and 1910—a period normally considered to be very prosperous for New York State. Not surprisingly, the four fastest growing counties are the boroughs of New York City—and the Bronx wasn't even formed yet! (Actually, the consolidated City of New York, including the boroughs we know today, was formed by the state legislature in 1898). After these is Erie County, home to Buffalo and most of its suburbs. And then back downstate to Westchester County, which at this time included part of what is now the Bronx. Schenectady County, during this time growing with the new electricity industry, was followed by Monroe County (Rochester). Rockland and Suffolk Counties are both

**Table 3.1:** Fastest & Slowest Growing New York Counties, 1850-1910

| Fastest Growing | Percent Change | Slowest Growing | Percent Change |
|---|---|---|---|
| Kings | 1076.79 | Lewis | 1.16 |
| Queens | 671.16 | Wyoming | -.32 |
| Richmond | 470.81 | Otsego | -2.92 |
| New York | 435.84 | Livingston | -6.94 |
| Erie | 423.78 | Madison | -8.78 |
| Westchester | 385.82 | Greene | -8.79 |
| Schenectady | 339.99 | Yates | -9.46 |
| Monroe | 223.12 | Chenango | -11.75 |
| Rockland | 176.34 | Tompkins | -13.16 |
| Suffolk | 160.38 | Schoharie | -28.89 |

SOURCE: New York State Department of Economic Development. 2000

distinguished as suburban New York counties, with Suffolk County the only county not part of the Great Corridor. All of these counties were part of the larger economic system centered on New York and extending well into upstate.

In contrast, look at the slow growth counties. Lewis County, north of Utica and due east of Lake Ontario, holds the distinction of the only non-Great Corridor county to not lose population during this period. Of the ten counties listed, only Madison County is on the Erie Canal. And within Madison County, growth in the canal corridor villages of Canastota and Oneida combined with population decline in the remainder of the county to the south actually prompted county officials to move the county seat from Morrisville to Wampsville in 1907—much to the chagrin of those in the southern hills of the county.

The growth of the Empire State was in relation to the access of a respective community to the economic system that revolved around New York City's trade to the outside world. Thus New York, as the center of the system, grew fastest and to the highest populations, first in the city itself and eventually spilling into the surrounding suburban counties and overtaking once independent cities, such as Jamaica in Queens. The counties lining the Erie Canal corridor, being manufacturing centers as well as regional political and economic centers, grew quickly as well, but paled in comparison to the New York metropolitan area. Those counties not in the corridor tended to stagnate at their 1820s population, with particularly remote counties even losing population. The trends for between 1820 and 1930 are shown in Figure 3.1.

Of course, not all non-corridor counties lost population. But even in those regions where growth continued, it was often due to access to the wider economic system generated by New York merchants and financiers. This was particularly true as railroads became more widespread. In Table 3.2, the largest and smallest counties between 1850 and 1910 that were in neither the New York

**Figure 3.1: Average Population of New York Counties, 1820-1930**

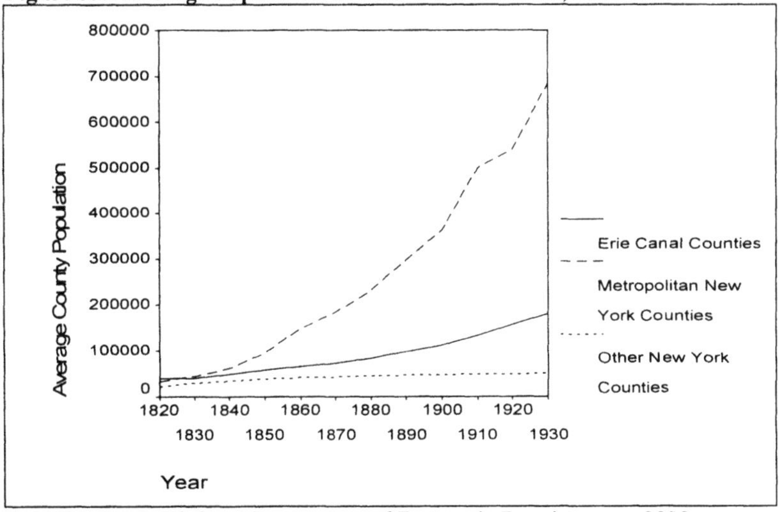


SOURCE: New York State Department of Economic Development, 2000

**Table 3.2: Most & Least Populous Non-Erie Canal Corridor Counties, 1850-1910**

| | 1850 | | 1880 | | 1910 |
|---|---|---|---|---|---|
| County | Population | County | Population | County | Population |
| *Largest:* | | | | | |
| Rensselaer | 73363 | Rensselaer | 115328 | Rensselaer | 122276 |
| St. Lawrence | 68617 | St. Lawrence | 85997 | Chautauqua | 105126 |
| Jefferson | 68153 | Ulster | 85838 | Ulster | 91769 |
| Steuben | 63771 | Oswego | 77911 | St. Lawrence | 89005 |
| Oswego | 62198 | Steuben | 77586 | Steuben | 83362 |
| *Smallest:* | | | | | |
| Lewis | 24564 | Cortland | 25825 | Lewis | 24849 |
| Yates | 20590 | Warren | 25179 | Schoharie | 23855 |
| Fulton | 20171 | Yates | 21087 | Yates | 18642 |
| Warren | 17199 | Schuyler | 18842 | Schuyler | 14004 |
| Hamilton | 2188 | Hamilton | 3923 | Hamilton | 4370 |

SOURCE: New York State Department of Economic Development, 2000

metropolitan area nor the Erie Canal corridor are shown with their respective populations.

Rensselaer County is directly across the river from Albany, and thus is functionally across the river from communities through which the Erie Canal did pass as it entered the Hudson Valley. Cities like Troy and Rensselaer benefited from this position, even competing directly against Albany, Watervliet, and Cohoes for Hudson River traffic before making the final entrance into the Erie Canal or Champlain Canal that went north to Lake Champlain, Montreal and beyond. Similarly, Oswego County is at the outlet of the Oswego River and the Oswego Canal, which connected the Erie Canal in Syracuse to Lake Ontario. Ulster County too is in the Hudson Valley and is home to Kingston. As for the others, large land areas account for the high populations. Saint Lawrence County, for instance, is geographically larger than the state of Rhode Island.

As for the smallest counties, they each have in common the feature of being quite remote. Hamilton County—by far the least populous county in the state—is nestled in the heart of the Adirondacks, and even today can be a challenge to reach. Lewis, Warren, and Fulton counties are each on the border of the Adirondack Park and to the north of the Erie Canal corridor. Fulton County grew considerably, however, after the arrival of the railroad helped to connect its twin cities of Gloversville and Johnstown to the canal corridor only a short distance away, and the two communities became centers of the leather industry. Schoharie County had roughly the same disadvantages as the Adirondack counties, except it is in the Catskills. And Yates and Schuyler counties are both rather small southern tier and Finger Lakes counties.

## The Empire State

By the 1950s, New York's economy was a powerhouse. Students in New York's public schools learned that eventually the entire Erie Canal corridor would be one long string of cities and towns, and the distant suburbs of New York would eventually meet those of Albany. From Buffalo to the Long Island suburbs, New York's manufacturing economy was creating the wealthiest society in human history, and the period after World War II witnessed the continuation of the high tech trend. In Rochester, Kodak cameras and film were the standard of the photography industry; in Schenectady, General Electric's various consumer products were red hot; in Syracuse, Carrier air conditioners were cool. In Utica, Sperry Rand was producing the first commercially available computer ever—the Univac File Computer. Soon, upstart International Business Machines, another New York Corporation, would create new competition. Aerospace grew in nearly every upstate metropolitan area, whether for the military or for civilian uses. But there were omens on the horizon; no, the omens had already been around for a while. It's just that nobody wanted to see them for what they were (Thomas, 2003).

There is a basic fact of capitalism that we all think we know: there are booms and there are busts. There are ups and downs, good times and bad times. And if in a bad time, just hold on a little longer and eventually things will come around. This is a basic belief that most of us share about how the economy operates—sometimes it's right, and sometimes it's wrong.

It is right at times because sometimes a recession is caused by the ordinary functioning of the business cycle. The business cycle is fairly straightforward. Demand for a product is growing, so companies producing the product ramp up production in order to meet demand. At some point, however, and for a variety of reasons, demand levels off or even declines a little, but companies keep producing and soon an oversupply of the product creates pressure for lower prices. Companies respond by lowering the supply of the product by cutting production, which then reinforces a dynamic wherein people buy less, thus lowering demand. Eventually, any excess inventory is sold to the point where demand again outstrips supply, and production (and workers) gets moving again. So, yes, things get slow and then recover. The system works.

But then again, there are other reasons for economic conditions that appear to be recessions but are more permanent in nature. We call these structural reasons, because they reflect a more permanent change in the way the economy is operating. And these, too, are endemic to a capitalist economy.

Consider our nineteenth century farmers. Early in the century, our Yankee immigrants moved to upstate New York with the vision of being fairly independent. They would grow their own food, they would make their own supplies, and they would build communities that were relatively autonomous from the outside world. Yes, they traded with the outside world, but each small farming community could have been independent if need be. And Yankee culture stressed this: to work hard, remain sober and avoid temptation, and be as self-sufficient as possible—all core American values even today. But as the nineteenth century continued, more and more farmers produced not for subsistence but on a more capitalistic model. That is, they produced crops with high market value for sale, and often bought much of their food and manufactured goods with the money they earned. This helped the cities to grow and integrated the countryside into the larger system. It also exposed farmers to considerably more risk, even if the risk was caused by the greater benefits of the "new economy."

In upstate New York, particularly in an arch from the Catskill Mountains to the hills south of Lake Ontario, New York farmers in the mid and late nineteenth century began to grow ever increasing amounts of hops. Hops could be used in a number of ways, but many of us enjoy them the most in the form of beer. Hops could be sold for cash to merchants who then sold them to urban breweries. However, during the 1880s, an infection began to cause a blight on the hops crop, and by the end of the crisis much of the hops industry itself had moved west to the more environmentally favorable and less expensive territory west of the Rockies. In New York, farmers were eventually forced to get out of the hops industry even with a ready market nearby. The decline, however, was not so much overproduction, but rather it was environmental (the infection) and economic (competition from the west). What might have appeared as a brief recession in the beginning was actually a structural shift in the hops industry as a whole, and New York was left out in the cold. Such structural shifts are not limited to agriculture. As we will see in chapter four, manufacturing has suffered similar dynamics.

Suffice it to say, however, that the post World War II economy in New York looked very promising. Aerospace was a promising industry after the war, and New York did quite well for a while, but states like Washington and California also did quite well. Well, no, cities like Los Angeles and Seattle did quite well, and they ultimately out-competed New York for dominance in aerospace. Los Angeles is a major city with universities like Cal Tech and UCLA; Seattle is home to Boeing and the market power it represented. New York had numerous smaller firms spread in multiple manufacturing cities across the state, and only a handful of universities actually looking at such technologies—especially upstate. But the big disappointment is not in aerospace, but in computers.

As firms like IBM and Sperry-Rand (now Unisys) fought for the business market in New York, other states were taking a more active role. In North Carolina, the state invested millions of dollars in Research Triangle Park—a complex of research and technology centers near the state's top universities, such as Duke University and the University of North Carolina at Chapel Hill. There was no such investment in New York on a par with Research Triangle Park. In California and Massachusetts, dense agglomerations of research universities in the San Francisco Bay area and metro Boston similarly attracted top scientists and other researchers. In New York, such an agglomeration of research was found in the New York metropolitan area, and it has done well as the economy has come to rely so much more on the "knowledge industries" that lead to technological and economic innovation.

Upstate, however, had an admirable collection of four-year liberal arts colleges and a handful of research universities, but these were spread miles apart and there was comparatively little communication among them. Simply stated, when the computer industry was here, upstate New York did not have the educational infrastructure to keep it here and so it was lost. For the most part, this is still the basic infrastructure of higher education today: many small liberal arts colleges, but without the research concentrated in the major cities that is found in high technology havens like the Rt. 128 Corridor (Boston), Silicon Valley (San Francisco Bay), or Research Triangle Park, upstate has been more slow to adapt. The notable exception: Tech Valley, an initiative among 19 counties in eastern New York, has been using its advantages in education and transportation to sell itself as a "robust business environment built on an innovative, educated work force, government investment in facilities and research, strong investment climate and various state and local incentive plans to assist businesses in all stages of development" (Tech Valley, 2008).

As manufacturing has been trickling out of the state, particularly upstate, the "new economy" has planted a few aberrant seeds but no garden. And the response has been remarkably similar over the past several decades, regardless of which party holds power or which personality holds the throttle. We'll lower taxes, sometimes directly and sometimes by creating special zones where taxes are super low in order to compete against low tax states like Texas and Alabama. There is danger in this approach—do you really want the school performance or environmental record of these places? For most of us, the answer is no. But regardless of how you feel on this issue, it's not the taxes that give them the advantage. It's the labor cost—how much less are you willing to make in order to compete against Mississippi? Or to compete against Mexico? Or China? Shouldn't progress mean that things get better for the average individual?

## A Different Model

We seem content to look to the places where growth is highest and assume we need to do what they do. We call this method names like "best practices," where we assume that if one place—be it a country or a state or even a city—is doing well, then emulating that place will help us to do well. But there are serious flaws with this method, and it starts with the simple acknowledgement that not all places are the same. Often, places that grow rapidly do so because they must also build an entire infrastructure. When Las Vegas grows, it not only expands over larger distances but it must build new schools, sewer and water pipes, telephone lines—you name it—at the same time and people to do so. That takes resources, and it makes the bottom line look better. New York desperately needs to upgrade its infrastructure, but we do not need a new infrastructure. We have one. Similarly, when the Maquiladaros of Mexico or the slums of China attract new industry, it is because they have the poverty wages and terrible environmental conditions that New York struggled for decades to overcome. When Mississippi boasts of low taxes, it is at the expense of public services that most New Yorkers consider central to a high standard of living—good schools, paved roads, and so on. Simply stated, we've been through these phases before, and we overcame them.

New York has a mature economy, and the idea of emulating the development policies of Mexico or China would be turning back the clock. And when we try to compete against states like South Carolina or Louisiana on their own terms, we start down that path. The answer for New York is not to be found in the states that started their own industrial development in this century. The answer for New York is to look to places that industrialized at the same time we did. Don't look to Mississippi, but to Massachusetts. Don't look to Guatemala, but to Germany.

The idea is not to emulate other mature economies because—once again—we are not the same. There are differences, such as the fact that we owe our allegiance to the national government and Germany *is* a national government. But we should look to other mature economies to see how they handled new competition, increased costs, and slowing growth. We can start by asking why England, well, still exists, even though they developed before us and why they continue to do reasonably well. Or why Sweden and Norway, both less populous and much colder than New York, have better access to health care. Or why nearly every working European works less per week than nearly every New Yorker. The goal should be to find the conditions that will make tomorrow's society work, so that we are not emulating but we are innovating. Just as New Yorkers did when they built the Erie Canal.

## Lessons from Clinton's Ditch

It is safe, although quite possibly controversial, to say that the Erie Canal could not be built today. It is not simply a matter of economics, political leadership or environmental concerns; it is a matter of New York being a very different society with a very different culture today compared to the past. Gone are the days of taking such large chances—if a Cost-Benefit Analysis does not show a profit in five years, we probably won't bother. If it sounds like change will be required or even just be a byproduct, we'll argue but won't act.

The Erie Canal was possible not only because of the economics of the state's investment—indeed, it was a questionable investment to many of its opponents at the time—but because of the other features of New York society in the early nineteenth century. As discussed earlier, the environmental conditions made the canal possible from a technical standpoint, but the culture of New York helped people dream a future with the canal. Eastern New York was "civilization," with New York City assuming the mantle of largest city in the United States in 1790 and such cities as Albany and Kingston being bastions of settled life. To the west was the great frontier, and it attracted not only New Yorkers but aspiring farmers from New England. The cultural emphasis was on the romanticism of frontier life, later to be sold so well by authors such as James Fenimore Cooper, and taming the new country. Such a culture of expansionism had already led to the state sponsoring toll roads such as the Catskill Turnpike and the Genesee Highway, and it was this same spirit that ignited enthusiasm for the Erie Canal. There is simply no cultural equivalent for the spirit of the frontier in New York today. The wider culture of the late eighteenth and early nineteenth century helped build enthusiasm for a project such as the Erie Canal, one that enabled political leaders of the day to debate and ultimately make such plans. DeWitt Clinton had a mandate, even as controversial as it was in some quarters. What is the mandate today?

As we noted in chapter two, New York is in need of governmental reform and a tighter integration of its communities to one another, particularly upstate and downstate. Just as state leaders needed to do in the early nineteenth century, what is needed today is a fresh assessment of the issues affecting upstate communities. We need to consider these issues from a holistic perspective, examining the political, economic, cultural and environmental conditions that have prevailed in recent years, and use this knowledge to consider a way back to prosperity. In the next chapter, we will examine ways in which the built environment of New York—its communities—have been restructured.

# In the Name of Progress 4

The major trend in New York communities, as well as those in the rest of the United States, since World War II is the increasing dominance of the automobile and the accompanying rise of the suburbs as the major economic and cultural force. The automobile is not the only "suburbanizing" technology, however, as the airplane also siphoned activity from city and village centers to the outskirts, connected by ribbons of new highway. As in other states, New York has witnessed phenomenal growth in the suburbs and outskirts of cities and towns, but this "progress" has come with a price.

## Car Culture

From the birth of the steam engine the dream of mechanized transportation had become the draw of inventors everywhere. The first step in this direction was the train, the forerunners of which were horse drawn trams in Germany in the mid-sixteenth century and the steam locomotives in England during the late eighteenth century. By the end of the nineteenth century, however, a more individualized alternative that did not require tracks was spreading among the very wealthy: the automobile (Kimes, 2004).

The first practical automobile was built by Gottlieb Daimler and Wilhelm Maybach in 1889, but it was originally the exclusive privilege of the upper class. Each car was built by hand, often with fine wood and brass or even gold fittings, and as such cost an exorbitant amount of money. By the turn of the century, finding one on city streets was rather rare and owning one a real marker of prestige. The American industrialist Henry Ford changed all that (Watts, 2006). Although many people think of him as the inventor of the car, it was in fact the assembly line that made him a millionaire. Ford realized that each part could be built and transported to a particular point on the line, and a worker would attach that one part on a car as it moved down the line. As the parts started down the line, a car started to take form as each step added a new component. At the end of the line the car could be driven to the rail lines (ironically) from where it could be distributed throughout the country and the world. To this day social scientists refer to this as the 'Fordist mode of production.'

The brilliance of the assembly line was that it cut the cost of the car to only $850, well within the means of many Americans. Ford concentrated on the most obvious market for his car: farmers. Early marketing touted the car as not only a horseless carriage, but as a tractor as well. Running goods to town or quickly buying new supplies was now faster and easier—no horses to hook up and a relatively fast ride—unless there was weather to be considered. With no snow plows, the car was next to useless in winter, and with little if any pavement (even in some villages) a good rain could strand the driver in mud.

The answer to such issues required government action. Pavement was common in cities, particularly on major streets. Most often it was paving stone and brick, but there was some experimentation with concrete and asphalt in the $20^{th}$ century. Out in the country, pavement was rare outside of villages, and even in villages, the early nineteenth century had experimented with plank roads—wood!, with little satisfaction. The occasional macadam road—a trench with 6-8 inches of small stones that would compact into a hard surface—was also found. But the vast majority of roads were simply one lane dirt roads, or mud in the rain and sleigh paths in the snow. The answer to the road surface problem was the highway—a paved surface of up to two whole lanes.

In 1907, work began on a new kind of road: a paved 4-lane highway called the Bronx River Parkway. A year later, work began on the Long Island Motor Parkway. Motor Parkway was a private highway sponsored by William Vanderbilt II, and actually opened its first ten mile stretch before the state-built Bronx River Parkway. The road-building would continue through the $20^{th}$ century, and by 1930 there was an extensive system throughout the New York metropolitan area, a start on one in the Buffalo area that was never quite finished, and the Taconic State Parkway running all the way to I-90.

Even as the parkway system was built, other new roads were constructed. In New York City, one of the most powerful men in the city got that way by building highways: his name was Robert Moses. Moses oversaw the building of most of the metropolitan area's expressways and several new bridges and tunnels. One can glimpse his vision of the future in the Verrazano Narrows Bridge. The longest suspension bridge in the world at the time, this double-decker bridge is twelve lanes of highway—no trains, no pedestrians, no bicycles. Actually, this was the vision across the state.

The crown jewel in New York's highway system was the New York State Thruway, a forerunner of the Interstate Highway System. The purpose of the Thruway was straightforward: connect the major cities of the state by a highway that would avoid the hassles of city traffic by not being used as a commuter road. The Thruway would connect the expressway system of one city to another, the expressway system handling local traffic. So instead of driving thru downtown Rochester, the Thruway passes fifteen miles south of the city, exiting to interstates that service the suburbs. In Utica, the Thruway has just one exit for the city and one each for the eastern and western suburbs. At one point, a separate expressway (NY 49) straddles either side of the locally impotent Thruway; further east, it overlooks NY 5S as that expressway services the eastern suburbs. In Albany, the state capital has only two exits and a tangle of expressways to get you there. Originally, the Thruway ended in Suffern and did not delve into New York City. The building of the Tappan Zee Bridge carried it across the river and down to Yonkers where it becomes the Major Deegan Expressway, but there are comparatively few exits until you enter New York City. And the small towns along the route—a very select few received exits. We will return to the Thruway again very soon to analyze the impact of this design.

All of this building added up to a massive government subsidy of the automobile. There are many towns today where the lion's share of the budget goes to the highway department—particularly for snow removal. The pavement for the highways, the traffic signals, the signs—all of it gets paid for by the government. Indeed, if drivers had to pay a toll for every few miles of local street, public transportation, walking, and the bicycle would be far more popular than they are.

Another transportation technology that is massively subsidized by the government is the airplane. After the Wright Brothers' original successful experiments in 1903 the airplane progressed quickly. By the 1920's Roosevelt Field on Long Island was home to many milestones in flight, including the transatlantic flight of Charles Lindburgh. By the 1930s most major cities had an airport of some kind, and after World War II these airfields would be further upgraded. In nearly every case the airports would be the responsibility of local governments with some state and/or federal assistance.

The original understanding of the emerging passenger air system after World War II was that the plane would be a kind of airborne bus. A typical flight would make stops in, perhaps, Albany, Schenectady, Utica and finish in Syracuse. This system would require that every major metropolitan area get an airport of its own. In fact, many smaller cities also built airports for commercial air traffic so that flights were available all over the state. This is of course different from today as many fliers prefer direct connections and as a consequence smaller airports are facing considerable difficulty as airlines bypass them.

More recently, the federal government turned over another publicly subsidized technology to private business. The Internet was originally developed by the Defense Department as DARPANET. The original idea was to connect government and university researchers via the network, and it was basically little more than an email system. By the 1990s Netscape had provided the first internet browser and the pressure was on the Clinton White House to market this government technology to the public. The internet allows people to shop and work at home, spawning tremendous growth in the delivery business but requiring a new wave of investment.

## Progress?

To read the predictions for New York State written in newspapers and magazines during the 1950s evokes feelings of pride and the urge to cry. For instance, the Associated General Contractors of America sealed predictions for the year 2000 in their new headquarters building in Washington, D.C. (8 June 1958). Among them:

- Automobiles will not be allowed downtown—above ground, at least
- Low cost housing projects built in the 1940s and 1950s will have become dilapidated and demolished
- Main highways will be double-decked, automobiles above and trucks below
- Highways will be equipped with heating elements to melt ice and snow
- Business centers will be rebuilt with spreading buildings set in landscaped malls

Yes, their grand visions for today included superhighways with little traffic and self-melting lanes, of flying from town to town and even space travel. Rebuilt downtowns with lots of parking and gleaming office towers, shopping centers filled with customers, and new factories churning out computers and rockets. Many planners believed that it would be contiguously urbanized from Albany to Buffalo, and the American middle class would be strong (Thomas, 2003).

To live in the New York of today reveals something else. While some people and the areas they live in do well, others do not. New York has the highest levels of social inequality in one of the most unequal industrial societies on earth. Some metropolitan areas are bleeding population but, with high priced airplane tickets and limited rail, the emigrants are forced to pay more to leave. In areas more fortunate the countryside is being rapidly chewed up as houses, office parks, and shopping centers are set amid fields of asphalt and concrete. It is a far cry from the fifties vision of the future, and if you wanted to see a glimpse of the way we were back then you need look no further than the train station.

New York had been a powerhouse of rail transport.[1] The nineteenth and early twentieth centuries were a boom for rail, the speculation in new lines at times leading to boondoggles for investors. New York trains not only connected every city and large town to every other, but often connected places you would not automatically think about. In more urbanized corridors a multitude of trains was typically available. In the Mohawk Valley, for instance, the New York Central competed against the West Shore Railroad. Further west, one could take a trolley from the western suburbs of Rochester to the eastern suburbs of Utica—plus the trains if you wanted to travel faster. Main line trains such as the New

York Central and the Delaware and Hudson frequently met with short lines spurring deeper into the countryside. Simply stated, you could get anywhere.

The rail system was in most cases owned outright by the respective rail companies. For instance, the New York Central owned and maintained its tracks, engines, cars, and anything else you can think of. At times it would lease the rights to use the rails to other lines—particularly short lines—but it retained the property. But consider the heavy subsidies for cars and airplanes. Trucking companies pay higher taxes and registration costs than passenger cars, but they are not asked to maintain the highways. The state does that, including construction, plowing, signage—even picking up the carcasses strewn across the state by surprised motorists. Or think about airports: subsidized as they are by the federal government (air traffic control), state (access roads and construction costs) and local government (maintenance and day-to-day operations). Yes, airlines pay leases for space in airports, but this income rarely covers the costs of running the airport—particularly in smaller cities and towns. These subsidies to auto and air amount to a tremendous disadvantage to rail. Had the federal and state government chosen to do the same for rail back in the 50s—take ownership of the rails and license their use—rail may have had a chance. What did get done was, however, too little too late.

Not surprisingly, as the 1950s became the 1960s America's love affair with the car was chipping into the profit margins of rail lines. In any case, there was little attempt to integrate passenger rail with other technologies, particularly the automobile. It is tempting to think this the result of Americans simply preferring the car, but the technologies could have fit together better than we tend to think. Consider loading you and your car on a train in Syracuse and riding the rails to San Francisco—no need for a rental and you can still see the countryside. Prior to the federal intervention in the market, the railroads were left to fare on their own to try to compete against the subsidized car and plane. The railroads reduced the quality of food and sleeping accommodations, the amount of seating space, the frequency of service. They cut lines and sometimes just went out of business. In other words, just at the time that rail needed to compete better with improved service, rail travel was made less desirable. Just when new technology to create a seamless rail-car system could have revolutionized transportation, America's rail system failed. In many cities, commuter rail was taken over by local government agencies such as the Long Island Railroad and Metro North, and longer range systems were subsumed under Amtrak for passenger rail and Conrail for freight. Conrail was re-privatized, but Amtrak is still around today.

Compared to other states, New York fared well. Many of the freight lines continued, although at reduced service. Passenger rail continued in New York City, the Hudson Valley, and in the Erie Canal cities. In many states, passenger rail simply ended, as it did in much of the rest of the state. In cities and towns not in the blessed corridors train stations have shut their doors, sometimes becoming offices or restaurants.

In Europe and Asia, rail is still vital to the functioning of local communities and entire regions. Here in the northeast we can glimpse this lifestyle along the Northeast corridor. Served by Amtrak, the national passenger rail company formed to save the rail system, it is still possible to 'catch a train' to another city, and it works well with local systems such as the New York City subways and commuter rail systems. Herein lies the reason behind its success: rail works best in cities and regions with dense settlement and local transit support. In other words, rail supports downtowns, and in fact works best in places where the urban core is healthy. Not surprisingly New York City's Penn Station is the most utilized station in Amtrak in terms of number of users per year. The Albany train station, a tedious car ride across the river in Rensselaer, is the $10^{th}$ busiest station in the Amtrak system.

Beyond the Hudson, Amtrak is less impressive, and for the same reasons that plague the system as a whole. Amtrak has come under considerable attack in Congress for not being self-sufficient, although its annual federal subsidy of money is a mere pittance compared to the subsidies for the automobile and air travel. The result is that travel by rail is expensive, and is typically given little thought when compared to the airlines and particularly the family car. If you are willing to pay the price—and this is more palatable for a single traveler than a family—the service is not what it was 50 years ago. Many trains between upstate cities and New York City face a wait of as long as two hours in Albany in hope that another train from Boston will be on time and link (or disembark) with the first train. If you find a train where this is not the case, you are still limited to the same places on the Thruway. In fact, unless you plan on stopping in one of the major cities or towns Amtrak will likely require you travel considerable distance in a car just to get to (or from) the train station (Amtrak.com).

Not all issues with rail are the fault of Amtrak, however, nor its Congressional funders. In several cities around the state, as in the nation, the Central Business District has been so deteriorated that getting off the train downtown confers little advantage. As mentioned, travelers to Albany must take a cab or bus across the river from Rensselaer to Albany. In Utica, where the train station is still downtown in historic Union Station, the beauty of the marble columns inside give way to a drab streetscape of deteriorating buildings and bricked sidewalks. In Syracuse, where the Central Business District is relatively healthy the train station was moved to suburban East Syracuse.

If you are willing to leave your car in the public parking lot—most upstaters have little choice not to—or have a relative drive you to the station, the train ride itself should be comfortable enough. But not fast. In fact, the ride will most likely save you no time at all over driving, and may even add some time. In fact, given the long wait in Albany, taking the train to New York City only works well for residents of the Hudson Valley. If the trains ran at 180 miles per hour as they do in many countries, without a two hour wait staring at I-787 across the river in Albany, the disadvantages mentioned here would be trivial.

**Table 4.1:** Planes, Trains, & Automobiles

| | Distance (Miles) | Auto Time | Auto Cost[1] | Flight Time | Flight Cost[2] | Train Time | Train Cost[2] |
|---|---|---|---|---|---|---|---|
| Albany/Buffalo | 279 | 4:18 | 47.43 | 1:05 | 245 | 5:19 | 43 |
| New York/Buffalo | 427 | 6:43 | 72.59 | 1:17 | 177 | 8:35 | 78 |
| New York/Boston | 216 | 4:06 | 36.72 | 1:13 | 177 | 4:37 | 89 |

[1] Auto cost assumes 25 mpg auto $3:00 per gallon gas; tolls not included
[2] Flight and Rail tickets purchased July 22, 2008 for departure July 23, 2008, One way, One adult. Flights booked through Expedia.com; Train booked through Amtrak.

Rail works best in large East Coast cities, New York and Albany being two of them. The healthy city centers, mass transit, and decent service help rail work. In fact, the savings associated with not paying for parking in Manhattan and the convenience of not having to search for it makes rail preferable to the car. Not having to fight traffic from the suburbs or the airport helps too. What can we learn from where rail does work?

Rail works best as urban transportation. This does not necessarily mean that it can only work in big cities, but there should be a walkable downtown and good transportation. The constant trade and heavy traffic between New York and Albany is likely what helps the Albany station, for instance. But if it is not convenient, as in the Great Lakes cities, then rail service lags. The car and the airplane look better, and these are suburban technologies. Whereas rail can help downtown—at least where downtown is still healthy in its own right—both cars and airports draw traffic, and business, away from central cities. In newer cities, such as Phoenix or Jacksonville, the impact is less noticeable because they have largely grown around these technologies. In older Northeastern cities such as those in New York, the impact has been inner city decline and suburban growth even in metropolitan areas, such as Buffalo and Utica, that have been losing population for decades. By choosing to subsidize suburban technologies over rail, our own policies—federal, state and local—contributed to central city decline. But there's another culprit—us. Part of the enthusiasm for the car is known to each one of us—it's convenient and fun. Break away from city traffic and you can go where you want when you want and have fun doing it. So we should acknowledge some consumer choice at work, both in terms of people buying cars and demanding new and better highways from politicians.

Of course, whether by plane, train, or automobile, things are not perfect. As shown in Table 4.1, a flight from Albany to Buffalo takes only a little more than an hour, but you'll need to show up another hour earlier. Although Albany is closer to Buffalo than New York, it costs less to fly from New York to Buffalo. The train should be a good alternative here, but it actually takes longer than driving in each scenario. Driving costs less only sometimes, but we only included the gas price for a round trip. Add in the $11.65 toll from Albany to Buffalo, or $17.65 from New York to Buffalo, and the trip by car becomes more expensive. But notice: the train is always less expensive than air travel—it just needs to get convenient enough to compete against the car!

## Through-way

Another example of a good idea with unforeseen consequences is the great dream road called the New York State Thruway. Conceived as a superhighway to connect cities—almost exclusively cities—to one another, the Thruway opened in 1954. It has been successful at its stated goal: to usher motorists from one end of the state to the other without having to acknowledge the places in between.

Many of these places are small towns through or by which the Thruway runs. There are 10 towns of 1,000 or more in population in which the Thruway runs so close to the settlement that it has the potential to interfere with quality of life and/or economic development: Modena/Ardonia, Ravena, Fort Plain, Whitesboro, Oneida, Wampsville, Jordan, Port Byron, Phelps, and Clifton Springs. These places get no exit of their own. For instance, in Fort Plain the Thruway cuts between the village and its waterfront on the Erie Canal and Mohawk River, but the exit is 3 miles away in Canajoharie. So, Fort Plain gets the disadvantage of the Thruway running through the middle of town but only the advantage of having a Thruway exit three miles away. In Oneida, the exits are several miles from the city of over 12 thousand, but Main Street—NY 46—gets none. In Whitesboro, the Thruway cuts an elevated swath through the middle of town without so much as an acknowledgement of the neighborhoods it cares so little about. The nearest exits are 5 miles away. In other places the Thruway does have an exit but nonetheless has disrupted the character of the town. In Fultonville, it chops the village in half as an elevated highway, spilling an exit onto a strip of gas stations and motels by the river.

In western New York, the problem seems to reverse: the Thruway ignores places it shouldn't. The lone exit of Geneva, a college town of nearly 20 thousand people, is 14 miles north of the city line. It is not much closer to Waterloo and Seneca Falls, where one exit serves both of these villages. Taken as a whole, the twenty mile stretch among the three communities is nearly contiguously urbanized but the Thruway stays away from this area lest it actually have to serve commuters. It is only truly useful to those wishing to leave the area entirely.

Had the Thruway been built along the lines of other interstates to actually serve the entire route as discussed above, one would expect an exit for most state highways crossing its path, and most villages of 1,000 or more people would have an exit. In fact, many of the rural exits along the Northway or I-88 serve less people than that. Larger towns, such as Newburgh and Canandaigua would have multiple exits serving commuters in those small cities. When the

Thruway opened there were 35 exits between Woodbury (at Rt. 17) and Williamsville (Buffalo). How many exits would have been added in rural areas had the highway been built as other interstates? 43! And that does not include the exits in metropolitan areas.

The original concept of the Thruway was as a superhighway that would act much like an express train. This meant it would interact as little as possible with the cities with which it came in contact. By limiting the number of exits, traffic would remain low and people could get to other parts of the state—or out of state—faster. We just discussed the effects on rural areas, but let us not think that urban areas were spared. In urban areas, the Thruway would—in time—exit onto the expressways that did serve commuters, and as such an entire local highway system would be designed. The two exceptions were New York City, where the Thruway was eventually extended to become the Major Deegan Expressway, and Buffalo, where it serves as a Beltway before tolls begin again in the 'South Towns,' or southern suburbs. Instead of the Thruway, the South Towns are served by several expressways, such as the Aurora and Southern Expressways and the Buffalo Skyway, that run roughly parallel or as spokes around a hub to the Thruway. Indeed, the Thruway is almost parallel to the Buffalo Skyway and Rte. 5 (Lake Shore Drive) that runs only a mile or two to the west by Lake Erie.

The parallel expressways are more obvious in Rochester, Syracuse, and Utica. In Rochester, I-490 breaks north and back again in order to run through downtown. There are 29 exits, compared to 3 off the Thruway. In Syracuse, I-690 has 17 exits that run from the Thruway through downtown to I-487, but had the road been extended to reach Chittenango—a probable and almost obvious extension—another 5 exits would have been required. Instead of 22 exits, Syracuse and its suburbs have 6 exits. The Utica-Rome metropolitan area has two expressways running approximately parallel to the Thruway to serve commuters—NY 49 and NY 5S. The two highways do not link to each other, and NY 49 straddles either side of the Thruway for several miles. Between those two highways are 17 exits to serve the metropolitan area, compared to just 3 off the Thruway—and only one for Utica itself.

The one exception to this pattern is in the capital District, where the Thruway does function as a commuter highway. Well, kind of. There are two exits for Albany and three for Schenectady—all of which are for interstate highways. So if you want to get from I-787 in South Albany to I-90 by the University at Albany, the Thruway is your road. If you want to get anywhere in between, you're on local streets or driving around the city. You're also on local streets if you want to go anywhere between Albany and Schenectady, such as Altamont or Colonie or Niskayuna. So the Thruway is something of a failure as a commuter expressway—unless you want to commute a long way.

Curiously, the Thruway Authority has been examining ways to improve the highway through the Capital District. For instance, Exit 24 is the busiest toll barrier in New York State, a consequence of it also being the interchange between I-87 and I-90. In order to accommodate the ticket system, all vehicles wishing to exit the Thruway to take I-87 to Montreal or I-90 to Albany and Boston are forced through this barrier. The remedy: make the ramps bigger. Extend them out farther. Maybe add an EZ-Pass only exit for Northbound traffic onto the Northway. For the corridor as a whole, perhaps remove the ticket system and have general toll barriers similar to those in Buffalo or south of Woodbury. But in no case is the plan to make the Thruway a better commuter road by adding more exits. Simply exiting I-87 south of Albany and running it besides the Thruway (ala Rt. 49 in Utica) could add a commuter highway and maintain the 'commuter free' road as it is. The Northway (I-87) would then intersect with I-90 as it currently does.

To be fair, there were reasons for the decision made after World War II about how to design the Thruway. It was thought that commuters would clog the highway if allowed to do so, and they do on the Northway, the Major Deegan Expressway, and on the Thruway itself in Albany and Buffalo. The expectation was that a parallel set of highways would handle local traffic. A 4-lane highway would have served the shared suburbs of Utica and Syracuse, perhaps connecting to the Arterial Expressway in Utica and I-690 in Syracuse. Similar plans were found in other parts of the state. Planners also expected the growth of the early twentieth century to continue, not the stagnation that in fact occurred. Even so, it seems unlikely that a second expressway between Syracuse and Utica was warranted. However, that decision having been made should have inspired a renewed look at how to make the Thruway an appropriate commuter road as well. Instead, local highways were simply cancelled—I-690 comes to an abrupt halt at I-481, Utica's North-South Arterial ends in New Hartford but obviously needed to be extended past Clinton. Nobody ever thought to extend I-88 past Schenectady to Troy—or even into Vermont. Even on Long Island, the Seaford-Oyster Bay (SOB) Expressway doesn't make it to Oyster Bay. In some cases, community opposition killed the highways, and most of us are happy that I-78 doesn't cross Lower Manhattan or an expressway has not taken out Washington Park in Albany. In many other cases, it was money—or the lack of it. In any case, what will future archeologists say of our lack of resolve?

## Unintended Consequences

Was the choice of suburbanizing technologies like the car or the airplane a good choice? Certainly there have been problems with these choices, the decline of rail being one of them. What is curious is that even had those choices been the best choice, the implementation was nevertheless haphazard. The highway system has still not been completed; the tolls keep going up on the Thruway. In some cases the fault rested with state government, but not always. The Thruway was built before passage of the Interstate Highway Act, and as such designers thought its design best. They did not know that Republicans would push for an entire system of free highways that would reverse the expectation of self-sufficiency for roads like the Thruway. Similarly, when cities built airports they expected airlines to be run as airborne bus lines, stopping quickly at each airport. The idea of arriving an hour or two early seemed to invalidate the reason for flying to begin with—speed. If airlines would be airborne buses, then each city needed an airport. Had they known the reality of today, they would have aimed for economies of scale—large regional airports to serve multiple metropolitan areas, like Buffalo-Rochester or Syracuse-Utica. Predicting the future appears to be a game of luck, and you can't blame people for getting it wrong.

One aspect of the design of the New York State Thruway seems to have had a happy consequence: less sprawl. Sprawl is the spreading of urban or suburban development at the metropolitan fringe. Compare I-87 south of Albany where it runs on the Thruway to I-87 north where it is an ordinary interstate. From the south, despite the pull of the New York metropolitan area, Albany sneaks up on you—there's comparatively little suburban sprawl. To the north of Albany, however, the suburbs stretch to Lake George nearly 60 miles away. In truth, the source of sprawl is complicated, but in metropolitan Albany one source is abundantly clear.

Sprawl in New York is an increasingly important issue. It refers to the spread of development beyond the metropolitan fringe to include areas that had been forest, farm or wetland. Over a half-million acres of open space was developed just between 1982 and 1997—425,000 acres in upstate alone. And the past ten years have witnessed a continuation of this trend. This should not be surprising downstate given the growth of the metropolitan area, but the sprawl in upstate metropolitan areas—nearly all of which lost population—is surprising. That said, sprawl varies among these areas.

Sprawl downstate increasingly is sprawl upstate. After World War II, a combination of state parkland and city owned land around the reservoirs in Westchester, Putnam and Rockland Counties formed an apparent northern border for the metropolitan area. The complex of parks near Bear Mountain in Rockland and Orange Counties in particular have been preserved in a state that is so natural that the Catskill and Adirondack parks are comparatively developed. For a time this 'green belt' held, and suburbs spread into New Jersey and Connecticut instead (the highway and train system makes getting to those places easier anyway). Since 1980 in particular, however, development has leapfrogged over the green belt.

The fastest growing county in New York State is Orange County. Home to Newburgh and Middletown, the county's population was 140,113 in 1940—already higher than many non-metropolitan upstate counties (Census, 1940). Growth accelerated after 1950, and the county had 221,657 residents by 1970.

Since then, the population has grown to 377,169 (2007); increasing by over 35 thousand people since 2000 alone. The situation is similar in Ulster County, which has gained almost 4 thousand residents since 2000, and Sullivan County which added almost 3 thousand residents during the same time period.

The picture in upstate is similar, but lacks the impetus found in the New York metropolitan area: growth. As Pendall (2003) notes,

> Between 1982 and 1999, Upstate New York converted over 425,000 acres of land from rural uses (mostly agriculture and forest land) to urban development, a 30 percent increase in urban acreage. Over this same 15-year period, the upstate population grew by only 2.6 percent. As population growth has slowed, moreover, land consumption has accelerated." (1)

For upstate metropolitan areas, this translates into a dramatic change in population density. This is most apparent in Central New York where population density fell from 5.17 to 3.54 people per urbanized acre—a drop of 45 percent. Other upstate metropolitan areas also saw population density decline. In comparison Long Island had about 6 people per urbanized acre (Pendall, 2006). Nevertheless, upstate is still more densely populated than other states.

A look at what sprawl, both upstate and in the fast growing metropolitan counties, actually looks like points to the real issue associated with such change. In many suburban developments, lot sizes of one acre or more have become quite common. Such large lots are important as the average garage of today is about the size of the average suburban home built during the 1950s. Of course, the economics of this development pattern is simple. An urban house—not even an apartment building—of yesteryear would have had a lot of between a fifth and a quarter of an acre, meaning that one acre would have contained 4 to 5 families paying property taxes. This meant that the adjoining street would have 4 to 5 families paying its upkeep, or 8 to 10 families assuming that houses line both sides of the street. In our newer suburbs, that same strip of street might have two families paying the upkeep. No wonder so few places have sidewalks. Not only are taxes higher, but more space is required to maintain the population. Using the above figures, a densely settled town of 10,000 residents will require 2,000 acres; our less densely settled town of the same population will require 20,000 acres! And this doesn't include communal areas or industry.

Suburbs are not, contrary to popular opinion, the only places with sprawl. Less discussed but no less important is rural sprawl. Rural sprawl is found in non-urban places, and may metamorphose into suburban sprawl, but not always. Just as suburban sprawl is a consequence of the automobile, so is rural sprawl. But whereas suburban sprawl is often more dense, pre-planned, and connected to basic services like water, sewer, and parks; rural sprawl is simply the development of rural land without such other markers of urbanization. There is often a conscious decision made by residents and local governments to maintain 'rural' character,' although this is rarely well-defined. The result is often an amalgam of development styles, the best of which merely retains a rural aesthetic in an otherwise suburban or exurban economy where people commute to somewhere else for work and entertainment. This pattern is especially obvious in those rural areas in the path of the New York City suburbs in Sullivan and Ulster Counties, but is noticeable throughout the entire state.

How does one define rural? It could be open space with woodlands, or it could be agricultural land with fields of crops or groves of forest trees. In most cases, the bulk of the population historically lived in villages, densely settled (that is, in sociological terms, urban) surrounded by non-urban countryside. Central Business District's provided basic goods and services, a trip to a larger market town or city a rare and exciting event. By the end of the nineteenth century almost no such community could say it was 'independent' or 'self-supporting,' but the ideology stuck around. When people think 'rural' today, they typically dream of a house in the country or in one of these tiny villages, but the reality is quite different. Just as New York cities have lost population (except New York City and a handful of others), rural villages have also lost population as people settle in the countryside (Pendall, 2003). Often, houses are built on lots ranging from only 2 or 3 acres to far larger, but 5-10 acre lots have become standard. Of course, such large lots allow residents living a suburban lifestyle (even in the country) the illusion of rural life, but at a broader level this pattern spreads development far and wide, leading to higher taxes, higher property values, and less community attachment to villages and towns (Daniels, 1999; Thomas 2003).

In both suburban and rural contexts, residential sprawl favors commercial sprawl as well. The suburban strip is a familiar sight in every metropolitan area, a collection of strip malls, restaurants, gas stations and major shopping centers. In rural areas, these strips tend to be less diverse and sometimes disembodied from a village center. Such strips are typically populated by national and international chains that, despite some local donations, funnel their profits to other places. Every time someone shops at Wal-Mart they support Arkansas; every Big Mac supports Illinois. In contrast, the independent businesses (typical but not exclusively so) of older downtowns are often owned by people who will spend their profits locally. Even without such economic dynamics, commercial strips most often require more space and provide comparatively fewer establishments than downtowns, and are thus more expensive to maintain. And, of course, they rely on the automobile and its dependency on foreign oil to survive.

## Any Ideas?

This chapter has discussed many of the issues facing New York communities. Nevertheless, although it is easy to point to problems, the purpose behind such an exercise should not be to merely criticize, but to offer solutions. Believe it or not, planners and geographers have for years been promoting a more healthy way of building communities. In general, historic patterns of community building are considered safer and healthier, and this includes higher population densities, sidewalks and parks, and slower speed limits for cars. However, this should not be confused with turning back the clock. While older established communities do have a reason for historic preservation, newer communities could enact codes for building healthier neighborhoods along the same lines. In planning, the "New Urbanism" movement has made inroads for getting policymakers to think about car-free streets (with alleys and parking lots for cars), dense housing with ample public parks and other open space, and architecture designed to both ensure privacy and encourage social interaction (by adding a front porch). In New York, much of this comes under the Quality Communities program.

To their credit, officials in the Quality Communities Program and the Department of State have been promoting this vision and even putting it into action. But while one branch of government argues for good development practices, others undercut this message. In rural areas, for instance, the Department of Health recommends minimum lot sizes of two acres for new housing in order to properly separate wells and septic systems. While understandable from a public health standpoint—who wants septic runoff in their water?—such a regulation is a guarantee of even more sprawl in rural areas in the future. Similarly, although the Department of Transportation is much more receptive to community input than in the past, many communities still have posted speed limits that discourage pedestrian traffic. That said, speed limits are only one way of controlling highway traffic—traffic lights and four-way stop signs could also slow traffic through communities. One might argue that such measures would increase congestion, but they could also help revitalize communities by making them pedestrian-friendly. Not overnight, but in time.

If the goal of healthy communities is held in sight, then state agencies should seek out common solutions. If the Department of State recognizes a set of practices similar to those espoused in the Quality Communities program as positive, but the Department of Health is concerned about contamination of wells from septic systems, then the common solution is finding ways of delivering water and sewer service to a larger number of people. This might call for new and/or extended water and sewer systems, and the building of such lines could be used to control where and what type of growth goes where. Along these lines, legal mechanisms to enhance planning to build healthy communities are not always required by the state or local government. Comprehensive plans are generally needed for receiving state and federal grants, but are not actually required. Zoning regulations are so basic to planning that a planner would commit sociological malpractice to not suggest them to a town, but many communities in the state will not even consider having them. If we are interested in building healthy communities upstate or downstate, the state needs to take a stronger leadership role in this area. And it needs to be uniform from town to town and agency to agency.

You cannot turn back the clock, but you can learn from the past and try to make a better future. Simply reopening rail lines and subsidizing passenger service is not going to bring back the good ol' days. Rail today competes with a decent expressway system and airlines, and it does not do particularly well. But rail could help integrate communities across the state better, and as a technology that favors the types of communities New York has, we might better consider it. We can consider how to make a better rail system appropriate for all of New York—something where a trip from Albany to Buffalo would take less time than driving and not involve a trip to Philadelphia on the way. There is public support for such an idea—Amtrak will finish 2008 with its strongest ridership ever. Part of this renewed attraction of Amtrak is 9/11—since that gory day, lines at airports have grown to inconvenient and even ridiculous extremes, and medium-term rail is an attractive alternative. Of course, with gasoline prices nearly tripling since 2000, this has helped rail as well. That said, Amtrak and the commuter rail lines are still not faster than the car and they can be pricey. To make passenger rail a truly viable alternative will take extra investment to bring New York's rail system up to European and Japanese standards. The answer is high speed rail.

It is common for trains in other countries to reach speeds of 180 miles per hour. At such a speed, a train from New York to Albany or Binghamton would take substantially less than an hour. A right of way also exists between Middletown and Sidney, where a split to Syracuse or Utica occurs. In other words, the rights-of-way already exist to build high speed rail connections to four major upstate metropolitan areas from midtown Manhattan. Faster transportation to these cities would enable better integration of central and eastern New York with the thriving metropolitan economy. The need for a high speed connection would limit stops to about every sixty miles, helping to preserve the countryside and invigorating those communities with stations. As rail favors central city (and town) locations, it could help reinvigorate older neighborhoods and downtown areas. Want to see how? Go to the artsy neighborhood near the train station in Hudson. And at high speeds, rail would truly be an alternative to cars and planes.

It might seem "radical" to call for high speed rail, but increasingly world class cities have it. In Japan, Tokyo runs on a sophisticated train network that includes high speed rail that allows commuters to live well over a hundred miles from the city. In the United States, Florida almost became the first state with a line that would have reached from Tampa to Orlando and on to Miami. Here in New York, commuters already commute from Ulster County and beyond into New York City, just as the country's other mega-cities have commuters from 100 miles away (think Los Angeles). If commuters are given a choice to ride a train that takes less time at a reasonable price, or even move to struggling upstate cities where the cost of living is a fraction of that in New York, they'll do it. If upstate residents can take a job in Manhattan and keep their upstate home, they'll do it. If people are given a convenient alternative to live upstate rather than in New Jersey or Pennsylvania, they may very well do it.

Currently, the plans for the rail right-of-way between Utica and Middletown are to build power lines to transfer electricity from upstate to Orange County. The project will not result in added capacity, and as such will not really address New York's issues with power capacity—only shift power from one part of the state to the other. The signs sitting on the lawns of numerous central New York residents point to yet another "upstate versus downstate" conflict. A train, however, would integrate the region and eventually extend to western New York as well. There are two different policy options, one that will (and already does) divide, and the other that will integrate. As with so many other issues, we should come together—not split apart.

## Restructuring Communities

Looking at the past in economic terms, New York made the necessary investments in the infrastructure for new technologies: the car and the plane. Politically, the investment needed to be made. To not build New York's piece of the Interstate Highway System would have meant forgoing hundreds of millions of dollars of federal aid. Given the assumptions of how the air transportation system would work and the fierce independence of each of the state's major cities, it also made considerable political sense to build the airports where they were built. But hindsight is best, and in hindsight there was little reason, for instance, for both Albany and Schenectady to have an airport. Similarly, there was no reason for the parallel expressways through the Utica-Rome metropolitan area, and there was little reason for various airports in small towns across the state built to welcome commercial flights hopping their way across New York. But few people knew this at the time. In other words, New York's built environment—it's communities—demanded a different approach.

By making this investment in new "suburbanizing" technologies, New York was keeping pace with the new technologies in vogue at the time. But by doing so, New York placed itself on a level playing field with other states that did not have the advantages that New York had benefited from previously. New York communities had advantages based on rail and canal technologies, and for the most part they still do. Does this mean that the best strategy is to sink our heads in the sand and hope for no more technological change? No! But it does mean basing our collective investments—our social and economic policy—on not only adapting new technologies but in getting them to work well with technologies where New York is strong.

Nevertheless, a change occurred in America at large after World War II in terms of how community economies operated, and these did change the political, environmental, and even cultural resources of New York communities. Like communities across the country, upstate communities have experienced considerable change in how their economies operate. Such changes point to what is and is not possible in terms of government policy, and this will be discussed in the next chapter.

## Note

1. The following discussion is based on the following sources: Kay, 1998; Wachs & Crawford, 1992; and information from the New York Department of Transportation, the Thruway Authority, Amtrak, Metro-North.

# Dislocations 5

If upstate was in and of itself a state, only West Virginia and North Dakota would have showed slower growth during the 1990s and things are little better today (Pendall et al, 2004). The problem in upstate New York is regional, as much of upstate is part of a swath of slow growth running from Western New England to the Appalachians of West Virginia. As we noted in chapter two, this explains to some degree the meager performance of upstate's economy. Furthermore, this meager economy explains to some degree the troubling trends of population stagnation and even decline experienced in much of the state.

According to the Brookings Institution, "the economy of upstate New York, by nearly all major measures, worsened in the 1990s, lagging both the nation and its own performance in the 1980s" (Pendall & Christopherson, 2004). Total real personal income grew by half the national rate of 29 percent. Even when news for upstate is good there's a grey lining. Information technology grew to 28 percent of the economy, but such jobs in New York still pay less than similar jobs nationally. Healthcare has grown as well, but still pays workers less than the national average. Higher education is another bright spot, but graduates tend to leave once they have completed their degrees.

This sorry performance was bad news not only for upstate as a whole but for individuals as well. Personal income grew at half the national rate. By 2000, personal income was over 10% lower for upstate workers than the national average; upstate workers received less pay than their counterparts in other states regardless of race, age, sex, or education. Even upstate's well-off residents earned less than their counterparts nationwide. In contrast, the lowest income workers in upstate New York saw almost no income growth at all during the 1990s. And this was when the nation as a whole did comparatively well, before the recession of the early new millennium and the rise in gas and heating oil prices. As a result, poverty has been on the rise in New York, no matter where you are, for families and children. And the poverty that exists is becoming increasingly concentrated in the older communities both in the cities and in small towns across the region.

Yet there are areas of potential in New York, some structural and demographic, and others in economic activities New York does well in but has yet to reach its full potential. We need first to get around the charged language and rhetoric surrounding upstate's woes, and only then can we ascertain the issues.

## Beyond the Rhetoric

We discussed in depth one of the four myths of upstate decline—the fact that New York's taxes are higher than the national average. But it should also be noted that education and overall productivity are also higher (Pendall & Christopherson, 2004). Combined with the fact that the most well-off areas of the state are in fact those with the highest taxes, clearly something else—other than high taxes—is going on in upstate. Are tax issues unimportant? Absolutely not! But they are not the panacea that some interests claim them to be either. The malaise of upstate New York extends across state lines into New England and into and throughout Pennsylvania. Curiously, New York state government has little impact on those areas.

It is often members of the business community who jump to blame taxes, and it is often their left-leaning opponents who blame NAFTA. As discussed in chapter two, NAFTA is often a codeword for a wider regime in the economy where companies shop the nation and the world for favorable business climates, which often include reduced regulatory burdens, tax rates, and often governmental subsidies. NAFTA does not predate these practices nor the economic decline that its opponents often decry, but it is a continuation of long term trends. What both camps have in common is an emphasis on the here and now. This is fine if you want to sell cookies or cars, but a deeper analysis should track the life cycle of an industry from its birth to its demise. The case of Utica serves as a typical example.

The citizens of Utica received a blow in 1845 when the recent state census showed, for the first time, a decline in the city's population. With about 12 thousand residents, Utica was the 29th largest city in the United States. The city had thrived in the first years of the 19th century. By 1810 it was arguably the most important city of the upstate frontier, as noted by DeWitt Clinton in 1810:

> Utica is a flourishing city on the south side of the Mohawk; it arrogates to itself being the capital of the Western District. Twenty-two years ago there was but one house; there are now three hundred, a Presbyterian Church, an Episcopal, a Welsh Presbyterian and a Welsh Baptist; a Bank, being a branch of the Manhattan Company; a Post Office, the office of the Clerk of the County, and the Clerk of the Supreme Court. (Quoted in Ellis, 1979, 110)

In 1825, the coming of the Erie Canal changed the city's fortunes. The city had developed as the major trading center—and the last gasp of civilization—before the frontier. The new canal, however, passed through the city, robbing its status as a gateway city and staging area. Overnight, it seemed, opportunity seemed greater in the newer cities of the west. As summarized by Clarke (1952: 36), "canal boats which passed through Utica by the hundreds enriched the western counties of the state, but added little to the prosperity of Utica."

Used to the continued growth of Utica's first fifty years, the news from the 1845 census came as a shock to the local elites. Other cities, such as Syracuse, Rochester, and Buffalo, were thriving; why not Utica? Not content with such speculation, Utica's leaders faced the fact that the frontier had moved beyond the city, and as such the frontier economy was no longer feasible. Looking to the future, a commission was formed to investigate the emerging textile industry in New England. After traveling to the Merrimack Valley, the commission recommended textiles as a way to change Utica's fortunes.

By the close of the decade, city entrepreneurs had sold stock in the Globe Woolen Mills, the Utica Steam Woolen Mills, and the Utica Steam Cotton Mills. By World War I, even more had been added in Utica and its suburbs making the metropolitan area a global center for textile production.

Consider the process at work, for it was a different model of capitalism than that known today. Utica's elite, a hodge-podge of merchants, bankers, and politicians discerned a political problem and resolved to fix it. They studied the issue and looked for solutions. They then organized corporations to address the problem in part to make money but also to help the community. The process itself, perhaps due to the legitimacy conferred by honorable intentions, appears to have gone smoothly and was supported by a wide coalition of the population (Crisafulli, 1960; Ellis and Preston, 1982; Walsh, 1982).

The textile industry expanded for the next 65 years, peaking at the opening of World War I. As Bean (1994) noted, "by 1919, two-thirds of Utica's gainfully employed were working in clothing and textile factories" (216). The city was growing by 20 thousand residents per decade, lagging behind the western cities but impressive just the same. Not only was Utica home to two of the largest textile companies in the world, but it was home to such other companies as Remington—maker of the famed rifle, typewriter, and later the electric razor—and Savage Arms, the maker of the Thompson sub-machine gun or Tommy Gun. In addition, in the preceding decades Woolworth's, the forerunners of American Express and Western Union were founded there (under different names), and Utica may have been home to the first incarnation of the Associated Press (Schwarzlose, 1980). Its business leaders:

> developed means of transportation; constructed the telegraph system of the state; established newspapers; organized the Associated Press; opened California with the Overland Mail; created the American Express Company; supplied the country with textiles, clothing, knitgoods, and shoes; and were in the vanguard of the social movements for temperance and the abolition of slavery. (Walsh, 1982, iii)

So what happened? Sheehan (1949) described the circumstances as follows:

> At the time of the first world war the city of Utica was one of the richest per capita in the U.S. (But) after the war the tide turned sharply (and) the trek of the textile mills out of Utica to the south began. By 1924 there were only six (of 22 in 1910) working mills left in Utica, and some $15 million of capital was tied up in idle industrial properties. (170)

It should be noted that neither NAFTA nor anything like it existed at this time, so we cannot blame the demise of Utica's textile industry on that. At the same time, we can say that taxes were lower in the south. While it is true that southern states would often tout the lower taxes that does not appear to be the case here: at least, they were not cited as a major reason. Instead, the 'right to work' laws in the south—laws designed to keep union activity to a minimum—were the big attractors. Union activity had not only resulted in occasional strikes, but also improved standards of living through higher wages (Pula and Dziedzic, 1991). Nevertheless, the lower cost of labor and even taxes cannot account in total for the wholesale loss of the industry.

The new factories were thoroughly modern and air conditioned, usually with parking out in the suburbs of places like Greenville, South Carolina and Augusta, Georgia. But Utica officials would have worked as hard to keep the firms in New York; indeed, tireless efforts by Utica's political machine, led by Rufus Elefante and Charles Donelley, did much to revitalize the city as its industry fled. Transportation was no better in the south, and the market itself was considerably smaller. The textile companies could, and did, make more money in the south. But that was not the primary reason for leaving.

By the end of World War I, the owners of the textile companies had redefined the meaning of "business". In the mid-nineteenth century, the mills were organized in order to revitalize Utica. The investors would earn handsome profits, but a degree of community service was involved. The upper-class felt a sense of noblesse-oblige—an understanding that they had a responsibility to those not as fortunate as they. Like most other northeastern cities, Utica's elite lived lavishly but also donated large sums to such institutions as the Munson-Williams-Proctor (art) Institute, local hospitals, parks and the Utica Zoo. However, the community service went beyond 'things' and extended to keeping the factories open in the city. This is not to say that workers were always paid well, but rather that factories were considered city institutions as well as businesses.

By World War I this ethic had begun to change. The mills were no longer community institutions but were simply 'businesses'. The factories could be bought or sold at will—the CEO worked for the stockholders, not the community. In the early twentieth century stockholders agreed to sell their shares to larger corporations with the headquarters moving out of Utica. The effect of losing the headquarters was more than just losing some people, it also meant losing an advocate for Utica in board meetings. When production facilities were discussed, those in Utica were just factories—not community institutions, not historic structures in the company's development. They could be closed at will, for their use was not to produce wealth for city residents and keep the city afloat (as in the beginning) but to make money for the stockholders who could, and did, live everywhere. The effect of losing local ownership of production is a major theme in the restructuring of Buffalo's economy as well (Dillaway, 2006).

So, economic considerations were not the lone source of Utica's misfortune. There was an organizational attribute: the people deciding the fate of Utica's economic institutions were increasingly emotionally detached form the city, serving the 'stockholders' only. And there was a cultural component: from the executives to the stockholders to the politicians, even to many laborers, the role of the corporation was increasingly seen as a vehicle to enrich owners only, with any commitment to the community a distant memory. This cultural shift set the stage for the decimation of the city's economy after World War II.

Virgil Crisafulli, a Utica College professor, wrote in 1960 that "the decline of the local economy actually has been in process since World War I when the textile industry passed its peak of development" (39). The economic dislocations of the 1950s continued these trends. Thomas (2003) summed up the situation:

> The metropolitan area lost 8,800 textile jobs alone. Hardest hit were the textile mill workers, who plummeted from 9,700 jobs in 1947 to 1,700 jobs in 1957. As a share of total manufacturing jobs, the textile industry dropped from almost 24 percent in 1947 to just over 7 percent ten years later. As a result, Utica had one of the highest unemployment rates in New York State for years after the layoffs and would not have an unemployment rate below the state average until the 1990s. (39-40)

Indeed, one reason the unemployment rate finally fell in line with the rest of New York was the staggering loss of population in the metropolitan area, from 340,000 in 1970 to less than 300,000 in 2000.

The loss of a major industry would have been traumatic in and of itself, but it does not explain the totality of loss either in Utica or in other upstate cities. The loss of the textile industry in Utica is an example of what became known in the social sciences as deindustrialization (Bluestone and Harrison, 1982). Every major city in New York, even New York City, has experienced the loss of manufacturing. In Utica, the loss of textiles was met by a shift to such industries as aerospace and, interestingly, the first commercial computer in history: the

**Figure 5.1:** Textile Industry Employment in Metropolitan Utica, 1947-1982

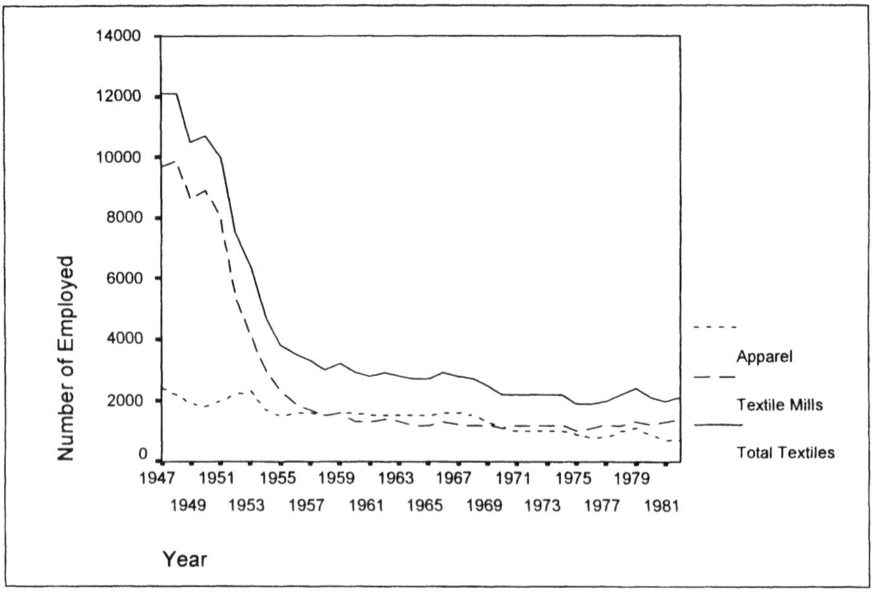


Source: USBLS, 1984

Univac File Computer. But as the 1980s became the 1990s, another wave of misfortune would grip the area. Much of the aerospace industry, for example, was geared toward defense spending. As the Pentagon encouraged companies to merge during the 1990s, the formation of Lockheed Martin out of what had been Lockheed, Martin Marietta, and (further back) GE Aerospace meant that operations could be centralized. Lockheed Martin executives, with little attachment to upstate cities, closed facilities in Utica and Syracuse. This form of deindustrialization was due to another recent trend: corporate concentration. Corporate concentration is the merger of once-separate companies into (typically) larger conglomerates. Most people typically think of manufacturing when considering such mergers, but the effects go beyond blue-collar jobs.

Returning to Utica, consider the case of the Oneida Bank. The Oneida Bank was founded in 1826 as a bank to serve the bustling frontier town that Utica was. One hundred years later, the only major change was a name change to Oneida National Bank and Trust in 1865. After World War II, as it became apparent that America's love of cars was leading to major lifestyle changes, Oneida National began to build branches in other parts of the metropolitan area so their consumers would not have to drive (and find parking) downtown just to cash a check. Enterprising managers realized that they could expand their customer base further by expanding even further afield by buying banks in small towns. In 1957, the first of these mergers was with the First National Bank and Trust of Camden.

The following year witnessed another merger with Rome Trust Company, followed by a name change to Oneida National Bank and Trust Company of Central New York. In 1976, the bank acquired Ogdensburg Trust Company and became simply Oneida National Bank in 1982. In 1985, Oneida National was purchased by Norstar Bank of Upstate New York, itself a product of numerous mergers. The headquarters was moved to Albany. Norstar was purchased in 1991 by Fleet Bank, a native of Providence, Rhode Island. Fleet later moved its headquarters to Boston, where it remained until merging with Charlotte, North Carolina based Bank of America in 2004.

The impact of such mergers was apparent very early on. When Oneida National acquired the First National Bank of Camden it was more than a simple financial transaction: it altered the social relationship between the two communities. Camden had been home to a corporate headquarters and the administrators of that corporation. The community could expect that these neighbors had a stake in the community, and that expectation was normally met in the form of not only corporate investment and charity, but the largesse of the company's managers as well. The merger turned those executives into managers, with major decision making power transferred to Utica. Decisions as to who could get a mortgage or business loan, for instance, went to Utica. The larger organization necessitated a more bureaucratized system that ultimately led to our current system of credit scores fed by computer algorithms and equations—a system that does not necessarily check to see if you can actually pay the debt. Gone was the more personal knowledge of the customer gained through regular interactions and customer—and corporate—loyalty. At the time, the impact was minimal, but over time and across more acquisitions the impact of a centralization of both capital and talent in Utica took place at the expense of the little towns who lost their hometown banks. Instead of a class of bank owners, they would have less powerful and less well reimbursed managers and tellers. This would impact not only decisions by the bank, but the charitable and other community work by the local gentry. Until the merger with Norstar, Utica benefited from this situation at the expense of rural towns in the surrounding area.

With the merger with Norstar, the geographical and social distance between Utica and the headquarters of the new institution became greater and greater. Norstar was based in Albany as a district office and ultimately headquartered in Rochester. This left Utica some low level administrative and 'back office' work, but the big money went elsewhere - next to Providence and Boston, more recently to Charlotte. Could London or Hong Kong be next? Or perhaps an up and coming global financial power we have not heard of yet?

In any one case, the impact can be substantial but nevertheless easily absorbed. First National Bank of Utica was bought by Buffalo-based Marine Midland in 1940, making Utica the regional headquarters. In 1987, Marine Midland was itself bought by London-based HSBC. HSBC has its global credentials concealed in its name: Hong Kong and Shanghai Bank Corporation. Corporate concentration shifts the balance of power among communities. Where once a company was wedded to its hometown, today it does what it needs to do to make a profit. The headquarter cities benefit as they always have, but those cities are increasingly not found in upstate New York.

As with the spoils of Africa, upstate New York has been a rich resource for buying the brands and products known around the world. Those resources were taken from upstate to make profits for people in other cities, and they did so through their ability to make a profit by moving manufacturing to lower wage regions. No longer do Utica sheets have any tangible connection to Utica, and the jobs left by Bank of America are a far cry from the executive level positions held by the owners of Oneida National Bank. People often refer to Utica as a blue-collar city; and *Jenny* used this stereotype to ridicule upstate New York on national television. Healthy economies have a blend of economic roles for people, but in Utica the upper levels were skimmed from the top and moved elsewhere. As this happened, those who could advocate for the city found their loyalties with somewhere else, and the entire metropolitan area has suffered as a result. Utica is as typical an American city as one can find, and it reveals a distinct truth: cities don't develop as 'blue collar' communities, they are turned into 'blue collar' cities. It is capitalism at work, but it is certainly not the values upon which American capitalism was originally based.

## Who Grows?

One hundred years ago, Buffalo ranked among the world's greatest cities. The city would eventually peak at a half-million residents, a contemporary of Pittsburgh and Boston. The city was home to one of the famed Olmstead park systems, a bustling downtown and thriving industry.

By car, it is only an hour and a half to Rochester to the east, the largest American port on Lake Ontario and home to such luminaries as Frederick Douglass and George Eastman. Like Buffalo, Rochester was a large American city but, in the shadow of New York and Buffalo, was something akin to an urban little brother.

As in Utica, the end of World War II brought prosperity that was followed by decline. In the case of the two great western cities, however, it was a matter of timing. Like Utica, Buffalo was home to industries that loomed large during the industrial revolution, and for Buffalo the big game was steel. That said, Buffalo had a reasonably diversified economy, making everything from cars to windshield wipers to breakfast cereal.

Buffalo's deindustrialization was by-and-large later than Utica, but had roughly the same results. Losses in the steel industry, as well as the other industries gutted the city's ability to produce wealth. Over 65 thousand manufacturing jobs were lost between 1970 and 1985. As in Utica, people were forced to move. In 1920, Buffalo was the 10th largest U.S. city with over a half-million residents, but by 2000 only 350,000 were left in the city and the metropolitan area as a whole had been losing population since the 1970s. Many of the manufacturing jobs left were those factories owned by out-of-town firms.

Diana Dillaway (2006; see also Goldman, 2007) has deduced five factors in Buffalo's decline. The first of these was changes in transportation. Buffalo grew to global prominence in part because its position at the end of the Erie Canal made it a major port in east-west trade. The first threat against this favorable position was the opening of the Panama Canal which made east-west ocean trade cheaper and easier than the combination of overland travel, Great Lakes ships, and canal packets that brought traffic through Buffalo. In 1959, the opening of the Saint Lawrence Seaway system coincided with the opening of the Welland Canal between Lake Ontario and Lake Erie in Canada. Between the two new canals, ocean traffic could pass through to Lake Erie and beyond without coming anywhere near Buffalo.

According to Dillaway, the second factor was the demise of Buffalo's steel industry. Earlier in the century it appeared as though Buffalo would overtake Pittsburgh as the steel capital of the world, but a combination of mergers in the steel industry resulted in most of the factories being owned by out-of-town firms. This trend was further encouraged by stiff competition in the steel industry from overseas. The situation was reminiscent of the textile industry in Utica, with much the same result. By the 1970s these firms were restructuring or even closing plants in Buffalo and its suburbs, resulting in tens of thousands of lost jobs. Combined with other forms of deindustrialization, the metropolitan area was set upon a downward spiral from which it has yet to fully recover. Dillaway (2006) points to the "absentee management" of such firms as factor number three in Buffalo's demise:

> The disappearance of locally owned industries and Buffalo's subsequent reliance on multinational corporations contributed to the city's economic decline...Absentee ownership and the new global economy complicated the ability of local leaders to create or attract new firms and shape Buffalo's economic destiny. (33)

Dillaway also considered economic inefficiency rooted in "militant labor and high wages" as a reason for Buffalo's factories becoming targets of their corporate overlords. Buffalo's working class had done well through its unionized workforce, so well in fact that many of the city's industries looked to communities with lower wages. In this sense Buffalo is a microcosm for the state and region as studies have shown that companies often leave over wage rates and regulations rather than tax issues (Markusen, 1987). That said, taxes were among the issues legitimately brought up by company executives, as:

> It was known that the City of Lackawanna kept the assessed valuation of Bethlehem Steel Corporation "written in pencil" to be changed easily. Bethlehem's real estate taxes fluctuated each year, often paralleling Lackawanna's income needs. These taxes represented up to 60 percent of Lackawanna's tax base. (Dillaway, 112)

Dillaway's fifth and final factor is "competing realms of influence," which in practice refers to political and economic elites.

In comparison, Rochester is a city of contrasts. The city has also suffered deindustrialization, but managed to retain corporate headquarters and thus benefactors. Kodak and Bausch & Lomb still maintain their corporate headquarters in the city, although the workforce has been reduced. Nevertheless, corporate and charitable giving is strong. Deindustrialization also started later than in Buffalo, and as a result the metropolitan area showed a growth rate until early in this decade when the population started to decline. On closer examination, however, the growth experienced by the metropolitan area has not been in the city proper, which has lost a third of its population since 1970, nor in suburban Monroe County, where growth has been flat since the beginning of the decade, but rather in Ontario County. The hinterland between the wealthy eastern suburbs and Canandaigua on the Finger Lakes in Ontario County has added almost 10,000 residents since 1990. The result is a city with many of the same problems as Buffalo—high crime, population decline, high poverty, segregation and deteriorating infrastructure. In contrast, however, the suburbs have grown enough for the Rochester metropolitan area to seemingly counteract its inner-city decline.

Much of the suburban growth has been fueled by Rochester's successful transition to a service economy, bound particularly by research and academics. Like the Albany metropolitan area, Rochester is home to two major research universities (Rochester Institute of Technology (RIT) and the University of Rochester). This accounts not only for employment and an annual migration of students, but also public and private research grants and entrepreneurship. Combined with numerous small colleges, schools, hospitals, and other professionals, Rochester maintains a considerable upper middle class that has, by and large, moved to the suburbs. Buffalo has many of the same resources but not the financial and institutional wealth that Rochester has. Indeed, the only other metropolitan areas upstate with a similar concentration is the Capital District and Ithaca—home to Cornell University.

We see this same trend in regions that do not perform well. A community with institutions that integrate the local economy with the global economy—what Thomas (2003) called 'unique institutions'—performs better both socially and economically than those without. Technically, nearly every community has some such institutions—schools and post offices quality—but truly integrative institutions typically involve considerable proportions of the local economy. In central New York, a region that has suffered considerable population loss, two towns that are similar in population, demographics, and history differ on this key aspect: Oneonta and Little Falls.

## Oneonta and Little Falls

In east central New York there are two towns each of about the same size, located on rivers and railroad lines, and with an east-west interstate. Each grew around industry through immigration, and each today appears to be an 'all-American' small town.

Little Falls is a typical small city in upstate New York. The city is located at the point where the Mohawk River descends 40 feet through rapids and falls (hence Little Falls). The location was thus a point where frontier travelers would dislodge and carry their boats around the falls. As early as the 1790s attempts were made to build a canal around the rapids, but it was not until the Erie Canal was completed in 1825 that a water route around the falls was an actuality.

Little Falls grew with the rest of the upper Mohawk Valley, home to textile and food industries. Twenty miles downstream of Utica, the city was part of a larger metropolitan region but remained independent. By the 1950s, Little Falls was viewed by residents and visitors alike as a successful industrial town. A strip of mills and warehouses lined the canal and railroads with a retail district centered on Main Street a few blocks north. As urban renewal programs provided the funding for some realignment of the urban core during the 1960s and 1970s, Little Falls as an industrial town was the model. A new 4-lane boulevard was constructed on the railroad yards, the industrial 'park' to the south and downtown to the north. The block south of Main Street was demolished to make way for modern shopping centers with ample parking.

By the 1980s, however, Little Falls was losing manufacturing employment. Large buildings in the industrial sector were vacant, and the prospect of filling them seemed bleak. Local elites seized upon a new idea: the transformation of part of the area into a collection of antique shops and boutiques called 'Canal Place.' With a four lane boulevard cutting the area off from the historic downtown, the quaint shops of Canal Place are by-and-large cut off from the Central Business District (CBD), and the transformation of Little Falls that was supposed to occur has not. Canal Place first opened in 1987, and is still today a unique and fun excursion, but it has not had the revitalizing effect some may have wished for. Besides deindustrialization, the city was faced with other issues.

Twenty miles downstream of Utica may have helped the region industrialize, but retail functions have tended to centralize in Utica's suburbs—not Little Falls. Several big box stores are located in Herkimer—six miles west—as well as numerous services and other economic activity. The result has been a general

**Table 5.1.** Number of Businesses in Downtown Little Falls, by Type, 1957 & 2006

| Number in 1957 (%) | | Number in 2006 (%) |
|---|---|---|
| 22 (47.8) | *Basic Retail* | 16 (31.4) |
| 6 (13.0) | *Specialty Retail* | 10 (19.6) |
| 8 (17.4) | *General Services* | 12 (23.5) |
| 2 (4.3) | *General Entertainment* | 7 (13.7) |
| 1 (2.2) | *Adult Entertainment* | 2 (3.9) |
| 7 (15.2) | *Civic Institutional* | 4 (7.8) |
| **46** | ***TOTAL*** | **51** |

See Appendix for discussion of Research Methods used in construction of this table

stagnation in downtown Little Falls. The city continues to have enough population to support its businesses, but the boom in retail and various services, particularly finance, insurance and real estate (FIRE), has made less of an impact in Little Falls due to competition from Herkimer and Utica itself. The composition of downtown Little Falls between 1957 and 2006 is shown in Table 5.1.

The relative stability still betrays a certain stagnation and even decline. In some cases, it is a failure to attract new services downtown—not an absolute decline, but a relative decline. FIRE services and education and healthcare, for instance, increased dramatically as a share of the national and state economy, and as such the stability in downtown Little Falls indicates an economic "failure to thrive." Basic retail, which includes groceries, clothing, and other everyday items, grew during the post-war period but then declined after 1988 as suburban competition became more acute. Specialty retail, items not bought on a regular basis, such as gift shops, also grew during the post-war years. Entertainment options—in this case restaurants—grew from four to seven during the time period.

The stability of Little Falls is a typical picture for many small industrial towns. Downtown didn't grow, but didn't quite decline either. It simply did not keep up with the growth found in many suburban communities. In nearby Herkimer, the strip through town witnessed new fast food restaurants, K-mart, Walmart, and a host of small shopping centers. In contrast, downtown Herkimer also stagnated as shopping went around the corner to the strip. In both towns, the real competition was with the new strip.

But Little Falls also shows what social scientists would call a 'generalist' strategy. City leaders had decided long ago that the future would resemble the industrial past. Urban renewal was used to prepare the town for an industrial future that did not materialize. When enterprising leaders acknowledged the deindustrialization of the 1980s as permanent, the tourism niche chosen was antiques—another sector with ample competition from other towns—and hence the potential problem with a generalist strategy. Because it chooses a wide niche with many players, competition is fierce. The potential market is thus watered down with each new player, and roaring success becomes more elusive. Little Falls is a pleasant community with the misfortune of competing against a seemingly endless list of other former industrial towns. The difference is apparent when compared to another such town: Oneonta.

About an hour south of Little Falls is Oneonta, once home to the largest railroad roundhouse in the world. The city sits off the north bank of the Susquehanna River. Originally settled in the late eighteenth century, it was the arrival of the railroad in the 1870s that turned the sleepy agricultural village into a small industrial city. The village grew from about 2,000 residents to about 13 thousand in 1930. Despite its small size compared to most major New York cities, Oneonta became a regional center serving the northern Catskill mountains and foothills.

As in Little Falls, Oneonta had a thriving transportation and manufacturing industry by the early twentieth century. Unlike Little Falls, Oneonta would also gain two institutions that would be relatively unaffected by the deindustrialization of the late 20$^{th}$ century. In 1889, Oneonta Normal School opened as a state institution to train teachers. The school remained small and focused on teacher training until 1949, the year in which the State University of New York (SUNY) system was founded. As part of SUNY, the now-named SUNY College at Oneonta expanded into a liberal arts college now classified as a 'Masters I University' by the Carnegie Foundation. With such an expansion of mission came growth, from 700 students in 1950 to nearly 6,000 today.

A second college opened its doors in 1928. Hartwick Seminary had been the oldest Lutheran Seminary in America when it opened Hartwick College in Oneonta. Similar to SUNY Oneonta, Hartwick College experienced growth after World War II, although it would remain smaller than SUNY Oneonta.

After World War II, Oneonta was the largest community for 60 miles in any direction—the regional market center for the Northern Catskills. Two main—even complementary—trends were evident during this time period. First, the importance of the railroad to the city's economy decreased, and with it the reliance on industry decreased as well. At the same time, the number and proportion of college students in the city increased, and with them the number of support staff such as professors, librarians, food service workers and janitors.

The growth in college students dramatically altered the composition of downtown. During this same period, when downtown Little Falls was relatively stable, Oneonta added 43 storefronts to its downtown area. Such change is not just explained by the presence of college students however: as a regional market center, Oneonta was the obvious location for a variety of stores and services if one wanted to reach the entire Catskill market.

Unlike Little Falls, downtown Oneonta doubled the number of general services businesses—including banking, real estate, lawyers, etc. The city gained in this market because it was the regional center, what geographers refer to as the city with 'central place functions'. In Little Falls, the central place functions were most often in the metropolitan center (Utica or increasingly its inner suburbs) or the county seat in Herkimer.

**Table 5.2** Number of Businesses in Downtown Oneonta, by Type, 1955 & 2005

| Number in 1955 (%) | | Number in 2005 (%) |
|---|---|---|
| 55 (34.2) | *Basic Retail* | 19 (9.3) |
| 22 (13.7) | *Specialty Retail* | 41 (20.1) |
| 44 (27.3) | *General Services* | 78 (38.2) |
| 15 (9.3) | *General Entertainment* | 22 (10.8) |
| 0 (0) | *Adult Entertainment* | 20 (9.8) |
| 22 (13.7) | *Civic Institutional* | 24 (11.8) |
| 3 (1.9) | *Industry* | 0 (0) |
| **161** | ***TOTAL*** | **204** |

See Appendix for discussion of Research Methods used in construction of this table

The other major sectors of growth in downtown Oneonta were in entertainment and specialty retail. Entertainment in Oneonta is fairly diverse for a small town, including restaurants, theaters, game rooms, and of course, bars and taverns. Much of the entertainment is in the form of restaurants, but the biggest increase was in adult entertainment. Adult entertainment includes bars and nightclubs as well as more lascivious attractions like strip clubs. In Oneonta, adult entertainment grew from none in 1963 to over 20 such establishments in 2005—the vast majority of which are bars and nightclubs, not strip clubs. The rise of a sizable entertainment sector in downtown Oneonta is directly, though not exclusively, related to the rise of students in Oneonta creating a rich niche market.

This is true in specialty retail as well. Specialty retail includes specialized shops where unique or niche items are sold, such as specialty gifts and art supply stores, establishments featuring exotic smoking paraphernalia, and certain types of athletic stores. In all, the number of such establishments doubled between 1967 and 1987. During this same time period, basic retail in downtown declined by two-thirds as suburban shopping centers and malls siphoned such retail fixtures as clothing stores, supermarkets, and pharmacies out of the center city.

Little Falls and Oneonta share similar populations when Oneonta's student population is not included. Located on the northern bank of their respective rivers, the two cities have roughly similar urban plans nestled as they are into the hills. The two communities even physically look similar as one drives through town or walks down Main Street. Why then the difference in the experiences of the center city? Two major differences are evident.

The relative position of each small city in the overall political economy is important. Based on the population of each city alone, one might expect each to be overshadowed by larger neighbors. Indeed, Little Falls has a considerably greater population within a 25-mile radius than Oneonta. What would seem to be an advantage is, in reality, a disadvantage. The distance to its nearest metropolitan center neighbors, each an hour away, forces Oneonta to perform the central place functions of a metropolitan center itself. The 'suburbs' of Oneonta is the logical place, and chosen location, of such 'big box' retailers as Wal-Mart, Lowe's, Home Depot, JC Penny and more. In Oneonta retailers, as well as the various services found downtown, find access to a great proportion of the region's residents. This position atop the regional economy aids its specialty retail and entertainment sectors as well. In contrast, Little Falls is faced with great competition in other suburban locations that not only attract the lion's share of the regional population, but much of its own local base as well. As a result, much of the external investment flows elsewhere.

The role of government policy in the institutions in each city is also important. In manufacturing, policies such as Free Trade Agreements (NAFTA, GATT) have not had the desired effect of increasing employment in American, and particularly New York, industry. We had noted earlier that such policies cannot be held responsible for the flight of industry from the state—the flight began long before. That said, such policies have 'rubber-stamped' an existing trend by making such flight easier and more lucrative. In towns like Little Falls and even in Oneonta, the loss of manufacturing is noticeable. In this case, government policy has not helped. Trade policy is normally a federal prerogative, and as such state policy has had to negotiate around a seemingly immovable force. The Pataki Administration, for instance, instituted Empire Zones—called Enterprise Zones in other states—that are now part of a bi-partisan consensus, and Governors Spitzer and Patterson have by and large continued the program as it was before.

If government policy toward manufacturing has not been helpful to communities, what policies have helped? Here is the difference between Oneonta and Little Falls, as Oneonta has the institutions that did benefit. After World War II, education received a considerable boost from both federal and state government. Programs such as the G. I. Bill gave aid to veterans to go to college; similar programs were expanded to other students as well (eg: Pell Grants, subsidized and guaranteed student loans). Additional programs, such as the National Science Foundation and the National Endowment of the Arts (Humanities too), funneled additional funds to colleges. The expansion of state-run educational institutions into a large public system like the State University of New York (SUNY) also made a dramatic impact. The impact of such policies in Oneonta was a doubling of (private) Hartwick College's student population and a SUNY Oneonta six times the size of its predecessor Oneonta Normal School. This created the specialized niche economy that replaced manufacturing in Oneonta, and there was no equivalent process in Little Falls. Can government policy make a difference—yes!

## Restructuring Communities

The restructuring of New York communities thus involved international markets and decisions by local leaders. What policy makers can learn from this is that government policy can influence a community's fate, such as in Oneonta where policy worked to its advantage, but also in places like Little Falls, Utica and Buffalo, where policy decisions arguably did not work in their favor or, at the very least, the communities were subject to wider market forces. This state of affairs unfortunately does not call for simple policies: one cannot say, "let the market handle it," because sometimes the market will deliver results that are ultimately at odds with building healthy communities. A healthy balance must be the objective, utilizing market forces while recognizing that they can be "tweaked" in helpful ways.

The major shift in the American economy since 1970 has been the relative decline of manufacturing and the increased importance of service industries. Services include retail and food service, education, and medicine. As one of the original colonies and frontier states, New York can capitalize on its historical and educational infrastructure. This will be explored in the next chapter.

# State of Learning 6

Education is important to any society, for it is the primary mechanism for transmitting the knowledge of one generation to the next. It is also a primary mechanism for technological innovation, the training ground and even the laboratories for scientists and entrepreneurs alike. Education often takes place in formal settings like schools and universities, but it just as often takes place in informal settings such as family rooms and tourist destinations. In short, education is the primary mechanism of both cultural continuity and change.

## History Revisited

Consider briefly the turning point of the American Revolution: the Battle of Saratoga. What is evident in the portrayal of history is a particular view of history. The Saratoga National Battlefield gives a balanced yet patriotic account of the several days the battle lasted, including the events leading to and from the battle. It is well done in an educational setting, and the hiking and car tour are unique and appropriate ways to enjoy the battlefield. The interpretive center ties the experience together, and veterans of all ages are memorialized in the national cemetery. Nonetheless, the portrayal is of a decisive battle amidst a bunch of other events—the flow of history as it unfolds, as one moment being a keystone for all that preceded and flows from it, is alluded to but lost. Consider the year as a whole (Savas & Dameron, 2006; Middlekauff, 2007).

In 1777, the British determined to end the Revolution by dividing the Northern and Southern colonies. The key to doing this was the control of New York, particularly the Hudson Valley and Lake Champlain. General John Burgoyne would march his troops through the Champlain Valley, meeting in Albany with General William Howe marching from New York and General Barry St. Leger marching down the Mohawk River from Oswego. Had the campaign succeeded, the Revolution would have suffered a major setback. But the Americans prevailed.

The Mohawk Valley was home to settlements of a variety of ethnic groups, including Germans, Dutch, English, and of course, the Iroquois. Tensions had been rising since before the Revolution, a consequence of an increase in European immigration to Iroquois territory. Earlier in the century Iroquois leaders had successfully developed a foreign relations strategy of playing British and French interests against each other, but the French loss of the French and Indian War left the Iroquois with only the British to contend with. A following treaty—the Treaty of Fort Stanwix (1768)—established a western boundary for European expansion at a line from Fort Stanwix to the Unadilla River and south to the Pennsylvania State Line. The treaty served to enrage European settlers who wanted to expand further west, an attitude that informed the Iroquois who their friends were (or claimed to be): the British. Not surprisingly, the Revolution would divide the Iroquois against themselves as some feared the colonists expansionist dreams while others thought them no less dangerous than the British.

Against this colonial backdrop occurred the Campaign of 1777. The British began their attack, with Burgoyne winning early victories. The campaign began to face problems in August, however. St. Leger was stalled while laying siege to Fort Stanwix as he marched down the Mohawk. When on August 6$^{th}$ American General Nicholas Herkimer attempted to relieve the besieged fort with 800 American and Oneida Nation troops, the British with their loyalist and Seneca Nation allies raided them in a marsh near Oriskany. The battle was a defeat of American forces that resulted in Herkimer's death, but the ineptitude of the British leadership first resulted in the Seneca leader Joseph Brant withdrawing from the battlefield and later the siege itself. St. Leger was forced to withdraw back to Canada rendering his arm of the campaign of no service to the British approaching Albany.

At about the same time, Burgoyne's force in the northern Hudson Valley was stalled and running low on supplies. Burgoyne detached 800 troops under Colonel Friedrich Baum to raid the American supply depot at Bennington, Vermont. On August 16, Baum was halted by the New Hampshire militia near Hoosic, New York and defeated. Burgoyne would not get his supplies.

On September 19, Burgoyne was growing desperate. His advance near Saratoga, present-day Schuylerville, resulted in a pyrrhic victory at Freeman's Farm. Burgoyne resolved to dig in and await General Clinton's troops from New York. After three weeks it was apparent that they were not on their way, and Burgoyne moved again. On October 8$^{th}$, an American attack on the British positions on the Freeman Farm under Benedict Arnold led to an American victory, and Burgoyne was forced to withdraw to the north. There he and his army of 6,000 sat as the American forces grew to nearly 2,000 soldiers. On October 17$^{th}$, Burgoyne admitted the obvious and surrendered.

The Battle of Saratoga convinced the world, most importantly France, that the scrappy Americans could win. This would lead to French intervention in the war and their role in the Battle of Yorktown that secured not just an American victory but American independence as well.

Some aspects of New York's role in the American Revolution might be uncomfortable. The Battle of Saratoga was a turning point, but not the end, of the war, and atrocities occurred on both sides. On November 11, 1778, British and Seneca warriors raided the frontier village of Cherry Valley. Over forty residents were killed, many of whom were women and children. The raid was in response to American raids on Iroquoian sites, and as such the brutality of the Cherry Valley Massacre was part of a pattern of escalating violence in the region. The following spring, an apogee of violence would descend upon the Iroquois.

General George Washington resolved to prevent further raids, launching perhaps the most brutal military campaign to be seen before Sherman's March to the Sea in 1864. Washington detached one-quarter of the Continental Army under General John Sullivan and James Clinton to "not just overrun but destroy" the Iroquois. Over the summer, Sullivan would work up the Susquehanna in Pennsylvania while Clinton would drive south. He first cleared the Mohawk Valley, and then marched overland from Canajoharie to Otsego Lake. At Cooperstown, he built a dam to raise the water level and then burst it to flood anything downstream. Over the course of the campaign, over 40 villages were burned to the ground, fields destroyed and warriors killed. The swath of destruction continued up the Genesee Valley, routing the Iroquoian homeland. When, after the revolution, Americans poured into central and western New York they were met by a decimated population with little ability to resist.

How does one turn such glory and brutality into education and tourism? By honestly telling the story and developing the infrastructure to show how all those events and people are related. There is a start to this project. The state has compiled a series of Heritage Trails available on the internet, although there is no equivalent on the highway system itself. It is a good start, but more can be done. Consider the New York State Museum.

The New York State Museum is a must-see for every New Yorker. It is on the main floor of a building best described as a 12-story psychedelic wedding cake at the south end of Empire State Plaza in downtown Albany. A relatively small space given to cover a complex state, the Museum is rather limited in its scope as there is not the space to properly tell the history of the Empire State. As Thomas (2005) reports:

> A perusal of the New York State Museum in Albany, for example, leads one through a fascinating exhibit about New York City, a reconstruction of an Iroquoian Longhouse, and a large area devoted to logging in the Adirondack Mountains. There are smaller exhibits devoted to the Holocaust and the contributions of African-Americans. There are large collections of wildlife and some mention of the geologic history of the region. All are necessary components of

> such a museum, but there is shockingly little about the Erie Canal and the cities spawned along its route. Given the centrality of the canal in creating the economic dominance of both the city and the state, this omission stands out as an academic lesion in the portrayal of New York's history, the neglect of the other major cities further stains against an otherwise outstanding institution. (188)

Unfortunately, roughly the same deficiency exists regarding the colonial period and Revolution. The issue is that the Museum makes little attempt to tell the narrative history of New York's development, and as such the emphasis falls on what visitors would like to see rather than on educating visitors about how the state came to be. The obvious answer to this issue is that the museum needs another floor to tell the story of New York's growth to dominance.

But why should the New York State Museum only be in Albany? Returning to the Revolution, perhaps a series of interpretive centers meant to tie together a bewildering array of national historic parks, state heritage sites, and local attractions would tie together the complex stories. Consider the Mohawk Valley, the frontier during the Revolution and the main route of immigration afterward. The region is home to numerous sites of relevance to the Revolution. At the western end is Fort Stanwix National Monument—a reconstructed fort in the heart of downtown Rome with fascinating exhibits and events—and nearby Oriskany Battlefied State Historic Site (with no interpretive center). There are other state sites, such as the Herkimer Home (in Little Falls) and Johnson Hall, home of Sir William Johnson. Near Fort Plain is Fort Klock, a reconstructed frontier 'fort' restored by a community organization. All, and others such as the Cherry Valley Massacre site, are on the Heritage Trail website. Beyond that, there is little direct coordination among them.

Now put it together. Double the size of the State Museum so it can represent the entire state. Create regional branches of the museum to coordinate regional attractions. For instance, a center for the Mohawk Valley, another for the Hudson Valley, etc. In some cases, an appropriate museum already exists, such as the Adirondack Museum in Blue Mountain Lake. In others, a center should be created in a location where it will have the most impact. An appropriate location will maximize benefits in an area that already has potential. For instance, a Mohawk Valley Center could be built in the (soon-to-be) former Beech-Nut Nutrition Corporation plant in downtown Canajoharie with the potential to revive that village's struggling but quaint downtown. The Mohawk Valley Center could coordinate with the State Museum and others in the system to create a comprehensive thematic tourism system. The Revolution could be presented as a fluid event responding to the pressures of the colonial period and leading to frontier settlement. Each individual location could specialize on what it does best, from the magnitude of Fort Stanwix or the Saratoga Battlefield to the quaint realistic populism of Fort Klock and the colonial luxury of Johnson Hall. Additional support to these sites, both state (Herkimer House) and private (Fort Klock) could create not only first class attractions, but a first rate system of attractions.

Of course, it is important to not inflict artificial boundaries. The system could include other themes, such as the Erie Canal (good museums exist in Syracuse and Rome by the way), industrialization, and farming, all coordinated and tied to the State Museum in Albany. Each theme would be organized by relevance, not geography. For instance, the Mohawk Valley is currently divided between the Central-Leatherstocking and Capital-Saratoga regions, introducing an artificial boundary that might make sense for funding but not for historic accuracy. A site like Cherry Valley, for instance, is more tied to the Mohawk Valley for its colonial history but to the rest of Otsego County for its subsequent years.

Given the importance of New York in the American Revolution, the high quality but meager coordination of tourism is a missed opportunity. And if one cares to look further there are similar such opportunities. But even in communities where tourism is successful, New York offers some hurdles as well.

## William Cooper's Town

William Cooper was a self-made man who settled a number of frontier towns. The first of these was Cooperstown, and long before baseball the village was making history. Writing about the trials and tribulations of this frontier village would one day win Alan Taylor a Pulitzer Prize. In *William Cooper's Town* (1996), he used original sources and the wirings of James Fenimore Cooper, reputedly America's first novelist, to describe the politics and problems in this mountain town. Long before Taylor, however, Cooper brought attention to the village by writing about it in *The Pioneers.* Upon his death, Cooper's grave became a site of pilgrimage by the well-healed in search of the wilderness. From such literary and bucolic roots Cooperstown became a tourist town, although the interested visitor may need to search a bit to find signs of this history.

The Cooperstown of the Coopers, descendants of whom still own property there, of graceful summer 'cottages' and of such sites as 'Natty Bumpo's cave' can be described as 'Historic Cooperstown'. It is the well-healed Cooperstown to which many of its residents, particularly long-time locals with upper-middle class standing, relate. You can see vestiges of this cultural concept at the Fenimore Art Museum, one of the world's best collections of American Folk Art, at the Farmer's Museum across the street, or the Glimmerglass Opera House up the road in Springfield. Area residents point to the well-groomed homes and natural beauty of Cooperstown as telling evidence of its historic essence.

Indeed, the perception that the problems found elsewhere are not found in Cooperstown permeates the community, although such signs that this is not the case are to be found. The school district recently added video cameras in the high school, netting a few pranksters unconvinced they were actually monitored (one child mooned the camera), and announced plans for metal detectors and a security guard supposedly to be in place by the beginning of the 2008-2009 academic year. Although this did not take place, it was nevertheless an indication that the fears of school violence that seem ubiquitous in the rest of the country are still to be found in "America's most perfect village." Add to the fortified school suburban-style strip development and a housing market primed to chew up the countryside, and Cooperstown is more down-to-earth than its appearances sometimes imply. And the more recent confirmation of zebra mussels in the lake seems to put the proverbial frosting on the cake. Of course, these are issues found throughout America and should not sully the village's reputation, but much of the area's tourism economy is based on the idea of an idealized country town and many of its residents prefer to think of Cooperstown as a village above such mundane problems.

If the Historic Cooperstown model is exposed as an improbable ideal by the sorts of modern problems that face nearly every community, that should not be a surprise. In fact, 'Historic Cooperstown' is, and has been, more of a cultural construction that has guided development and legislative decisions. It is the tradition that gives the village the aesthetic of the classic American small town. Tradition has become character through modern legislation:

> Ordinances were adopted meant to enhance the quaint, historical character of the village. The entire village was eventually designated as historic and placed on the National Register of Historic Places; vinyl and aluminum siding was prohibited from older structures; mobile homes were prohibited; and signs were required to meet certain specifications. (Thomas, 2003, 108-109)

This image of small town life was the primary appeal of Cooperstown's tourism economy for much of the twentieth century, although a new model became prominent in the 1990s: Baseball Town USA.

Baseball Town USA is actually a conceptual outgrowth of Historic Cooperstown. It is rooted in the village's role as a site of pilgrimage for baseball fans the world over, specifically the Baseball Hall of Fame and Doubleday Field, the mythological birthplace of baseball. In other words, it is rooted in the rather quirky history of baseball itself. In 1989, noted biologist Steven Jay Gould weighed in on the 'Creation Myths of Cooperstown'. He suggested that humans find it comforting to believe in a sudden, unique invention story over a slow evolution over time, using baseball as his guide. Indeed, the 'Doubleday Creation Myth' set the stage for Baseball Town USA.

Something like modern Baseball has been played for centuries. The British game Cricket is played throughout the world, and it too involves bases (only two), a ball, and a bat. Another game, Rounders, is more likely Baseballs' ancestor, however. It involves four bases, a pitched ball (thrown underarm), and a bat.

Its rules are similar to Softball. It is quite likely that any of these games were referred to as 'baseball' in the early nineteenth century, and that different rules were found in different regions. It is possible that upstate New Yorkers played by 'New England' rules due to the area's heavy New England influence, whereas downstate residents played by 'New York' rules resembling those we know today. If so, then perhaps Abner Doubleday taught the boys of Cooperstown the New York rules of baseball; and little Abner Graves, then just five years old, confused the issue. But probably not—consider the wider context.

In 1908, the *Mills Commission on Baseball Origins* published the results of a multi-year investigation that concluded that baseball was 'invented' by Abner Doubleday in Elihu Phinney's pasture in 1839. The claim was based on the claims of Abner Graves, who would have been five years old at the time. Although of questionable character, "apparently no record exists of any attempt to cross examine his claims." (Springwood, 1996, 33). In his 1925 *History of Cooperstown*, Birdsall suggests that the famous game never occurred. So why create such a myth to begin with?

The Mills Commission was formed because of a dispute between Albert Spaulding, co-founder of the National Baseball League, who believed baseball to be a uniquely American game, and Henry Chadwick, the British-born editor of Spaulding's Official Base Ball Guide, who believed it to have British origins. Chadwick described the dispute as "a joke between Albert and myself" (Levine, 1985, 115). Nevertheless, Spaulding created the Mills Commission in 1905 to investigate whether baseball was an American creation or the result of a long social evolution. The findings were never really in question.

The issue was not a matter for historians, however, as the committee was primarily composed of politicians, business leaders and former baseball players. Springwood (1996) noted:

> In truth, very little actual work was performed by the committee. As a prominent group of figureheads it served mainly to suggest a stronger sense of authority. Most of the official analysis was done by Mills. Spaulding largely controlled the flow of historical materials that came his way, and indeed, he seemed to draw on every possible shred of testimony, however tenuous, that might support his indigenous theory of baseball's origin. (31-32)

The composition of the Commission was thus pre-disposed to find an American root for the game, and by the end of the search only two choices remained: the precarious story of Abner Graves or the documented game in Hoboken, New Jersey. Neither choice was particularly attractive, but Little Abner Graves gave a more bucolic narrative than the documented 1842 game in industrial Hoboken. The story of a Civil War hero in his youth inventing the national pastime and teaching it to little boys in a pasture in Cooperstown beat out the organized games in the shadows of factories and multi-ethnic slums in Hoboken, and so Cooperstown was proclaimed 'birthplace of baseball.'

There was some interest in the findings when they came out, but nothing formal until the 1917 founding of the Doubleday Memorial Fund (Birdsall, 1925). They raised money to buy the Phinney Pasture and construct a baseball field. In 1934, the Works Progress Administration, one of Franklin D. Roosevelt's New Deal programs, built the stadium. And in 1936, the Baseball Hall of Fame inducted its first class into its home above the village library. The building itself was dedicated in 1939, and growth of the museum was steady after World War II. By the end of the century the Hall of Fame attracted over 350,000 visitors per year.

The Hall of Fame fit quite well with Historic Cooperstown. It was a museum, almost by definition a well-healed institution that purported to celebrate the birth of America's national pastime. Its non-ostentatious building houses a first-rate museum and a research facility. In this sense, it is similar to the museums of the New York State Historical Association—the Fenimore Art Museum and the Farmers Museum—and Bassett Hospital. It organized the annual Hall of Fame Induction ceremony and Hall of Fame Game, historically on one weekend, but now on two, that have attracted fans from around the country and even the world. (In 2008 Major League Baseball announced that there would be no more Hall of Fame games). The annual events were pilgrimages in the classic sense, on the order of the Greeks traveling to Mount Olympus. Visitors came from around the known world and shared an almost religious belief that baseball makes life worthwhile. They filed into the sacred village and worshiped at the local shrine—the Hall of Fame itself and its mission of celebrating the exploits of past heroes. The masses moved to the hallowed ground of the stadium for the games. Important people would speak, the National Anthem was sung, and the games began—a Home Run Derby and then the game itself. Afterwards, the pilgrims filled the restaurants and pubs to ply themselves with food and drink and relive the glory of the day, seeking souvenirs on their way out of town.

The masses participating in the ritual grew decade by decade. When downtown Cooperstown faced a downturn in community oriented retail during the late 1980s and 1990s, just as many communities did, the empty storefronts were filled with new vendors aimed at the tourist population. While many local businesses suffered at the hand of competition from the suburbs of Utica and Oneonta, tourism businesses thrived. The irony of Cooperstown's economic success is that while you can buy highly prized baseball cards and signed balls, a simple pair of cleats or batting gloves is difficult to find.

The changes affecting downtown Cooperstown have been the result of 1) increased competition in the locally-oriented Basic Retail sector, and 2) a sharp increase in the number of tourists between 1980 and 2005 (Thomas et al, 2003). This lead to a decline in Basic Retail, from 29 establishments in 1979 to 10 establishments in 2005, which were subsequently replaced by tourism oriented

**Table 6.1** Number of Businesses in Downtown Cooperstown, by Type, 1979 & 2005

| Number in 1979 (%) | | Number in 2005 (%) |
|---|---|---|
| 29 (37.7) | *Basic Retail* | 10 (9.2) |
| 15 (19.5) | *Specialty Retail* | 50 (45.9) |
| 13 (16.9) | *General Services* | 21 (19.3) |
| 14 (18.2) | *General Entertainment* | 21 (19.3) |
| 2 (2.6) | *Adult Entertainment* | 3 (2.8) |
| 4 (5.2) | *Civic Institutional* | 4 (3.7) |
| **77** | ***TOTAL*** | **109** |

See Appendix for discussion of Research Methods used in construction of this table

Specialty Retail establishments. Not surprisingly, many of these were oriented toward baseball. Of the fifty specialty retail establishments, almost half (23) were oriented primarily toward the baseball market in 2005. This has caused some locals to snipe about downtown being "all baseball," even though less than a quarter of the businesses were baseball-related. In contrast, as shown in Table 6.1, the village mirrored national trends in terms of the increasing importance of services.

When one considers the impact on the visual aesthetic of downtown Cooperstown, the conflict between two alternate visions of the community is evident. Historic Cooperstown is the vision of the quintessential small-town life of *Leave it to Beaver* or *Greenacres* fame. It was never truly a reality but rather an illusion achieved through strict regulation. It was nevertheless the way many residents preferred to see the village and surrounding countryside. Baseball Town USA was primarily a model of newcomers, entrepreneurs, and business leaders convinced that the old ways of the town should be relegated to history. Retail was to be centered in the strip malls in other towns and agriculture was in decline. Tourism was and is the future. This conflict between two competing visions was visible nearly everywhere, but played itself out primarily in the countryside.

A series of conflicts over development took place in the late 1980s, with the Historic Cooperstown vision often gaining the upper hand in the village (Thomas, 2003). Faced with growth restrictions in the village and adjoining town of Otsego, developers simply peered two miles south to the Town of Hartwick. Hartwick had endured several decades of economic decline in agriculture and in the retail base of its town center, and as such was more open to new retail development (Thomas, 1998; Thomas 2003). More importantly, the town had few regulations governing growth—a subdivision and site plan review law being the primary tools available to members of the town planning board. Town politics precluded zoning regulations (of any kind)—the preferred tool of planners—leaving the planning board with little, if any, ability to stop development considered undesirable by residents. Throughout the 1980s small businesses popped

**Table 6.2** Number of Businesses on the Hartwick Strip, by Type, 1997 & 2005

| Number in 1997 (%) | | Number in 2005 (%) |
|---|---|---|
| 9 (32.1) | *Basic Retail* | 9 (21.4) |
| 7 (25.0) | *Specialty Retail* | 11 (26.2) |
| 1 (3.6) | *General Services* | 7 (16.7) |
| 11 (39.3) | *General Entertainment* | 15 (35.7) |
| **28** | ***TOTAL*** | **42** |

See Appendix for discussion of Research Methods used in construction of this table

up along the corridor leading to Cooperstown, but it was not until the early 1990s that major development was proposed. Area activists were alarmed, and a proposed shopping center drew at least two different petitions calling on the town of Hartwick to turn down the developers. Without more stringent laws, the only option was the state's SEQRA law, the law that governs environmental impacts. Whether it was due to legal limitations or actual sentiment in favor of development, the planning board approved the shopping center. It opened in November 1993 amid picketers protesting the birth of the 'Hartwick Strip'.

Earlier research suggested that the strip would develop the retail infrastructure oriented to the local community (Thomas, 1998), but this has not been the case. Growth on the strip, however, has primarily been with specialty retail (though generally not baseball oriented) and entertainment—particularly restaurants. Even though there are considerably fewer businesses along the strip, it stretches for about three miles along Route 28 south of Cooperstown—a model of sprawl. Another fast growing sector along the strip is hotels and motels. Indeed, in 2007 there were enough rooms along the strip for 1,062 visitors, compared to 855 in the village. When all possible types of housing are included for tourists, including campgrounds, bed & breakfast inns, and youth camps, the number of potential guests in the town of Hartwick is over three times that of Cooperstown village—3,639 compared to 1,204 (Thomas et al, 2008). Increasingly, when a tourist goes to Cooperstown, they are really going to Hartwick! This tourism-oriented economy in the countryside has thus also assaulted the sentiments of those who prefer the Historic Cooperstown model. Even Wal-mart tried to cash in on the Historic Cooperstown model by airing a commercial selling the novelty of Cooperstown as an all-American small town even though the nearest Wal-mart is 25 miles away.

The case of Cooperstown should serve as a warning to the benefits and the peril of a tourist economy. Cooperstown is a tremendous success story of remodeling its tourist economy for each new generation (Thomas et al, 2005). At the same time, once a new spiral of development began the ability of locals to control what the area would become was lost. The image of the village as a center for the arts and history, of natural beauty and a pleasant built environment, has been challenged by the opening of baseball camps, souvenir shops, and other such attractions. It is a conflict that continues to unfold.

Faced with a governmental structure that cannot or does not supply centralized regional leadership where such issues exist, the area is fragmented into at least 10 governmental entities that are forced to compete rather than cooperate. They include the: Village of Cooperstown, Town of Otsego, Town of Middlefield, Town of Springfield, Town of Hartwick, Cooperstown Central School, Cherry Valley-Springfield Central School, Fly Creek Lighting District, Hartwick Lighting District, Hartwick Water District and a total of five Fire Districts.

Curiously, the growth in the town of Hartwick is outside of a light and water district, and as such local officials have discussed the future likelihood of districts for both! And in this environmentally sensitive area of the upper Susquehanna Valley, a sewer district would be a good idea as well. As most communities in this part of New York do not have sewer districts even if they have water districts, the creation of one should not be taken for granted. Needless to say, with such a complex of local government entities and private groups, it is not obvious who should take the lead in addressing regional issues such as a sewer. So, for the most part, nobody does. As we will see in chapter eight, this is a widespread problem in New York and not an issue that is unique to Greater Cooperstown.

## College Days

Tourism is a sector of the economy that New York does well, but does not reach its full potential. Another industry done well but with room for improvement is higher education. Upstate New York is home to 206 higher education institutions—there is a higher proportion of colleges to residents in upstate than there is downstate and in the country as a whole. Such a large number of colleges is responsible for one of the two populations that actually increases in upstate New York: college age students. Pendall et al (2004) found that colleges attract students from out of state to upstate. The only other major source of new upstate residents is the prison population.

After college, many residents leave upstate (Pendall et al, 2004). A certain amount of out-migration is 'natural', but upstate does not bring in enough educated workers to replace those leaving the state. In fact, if upstate were a state it would be last for immigration of college educated workers (Dietz, 2007). It is thus wise to consider what graduates can do once they earn their Bachelor's degree.

In terms of employment, the region simply does not provide the opportunities of other states. Many occupations are few and far between, and those who can find jobs make less than they would in other parts of the country. We have discussed these trends at other points in the book.

In terms of continuing their education, the 206 higher education institutions shrink to only a handful of major research universities where one can earn a doctorate. If you want a doctorate, your choices in Upstate are: the University of Buffalo, Cornell University, Binghamton University (SUNY), Syracuse University, the University of Rochester, Albany University (SUNY); Rochester Institute of Technology (RIT), Rensselear Polytechnic Institute (RPI) and Environmental Science and Forestry (SUNY). If you want to go to law school, your choices are Cornell University, Syracuse University, the University of Buffalo, and Albany Law School. Medical school is similarly limited, and even that Upstate stalwart—Cornell—has located its medical school in Manhattan.

This profile compares favorably to the Dakotas or West Virginia, but not to other northeastern states. To be sure, there are plenty of Masters Degree programs in education and business, but such programs, while valuable, are not likely to produce the same level of research and entrepreneurship as research universities. Entrepreneurialism is not, however, an easily pursued policy—it depends on a network of those with knowledge, those with capital and those with the guts to connect with each other. These individuals interact over time and eventually create ideas that over time create jobs. For instance, MapInfo Corporation in Troy was founded by RPI students in 1986. The technology was based on computers but ultimately useful in geography. The company was nurtured by the university and Rensselear County Economic Development officials and today is a global corporation with revenues of $165.5 Million in 2006 (MapInfo, 2007; Dressel, 1999). In places like Cornell University's Business and Technology Park and other similar entities at other major universities, there may be more MapInfos[1]. What is being done is good, but it is not enough.

New York could encourage economic growth by encouraging more graduate level institutions, both in the private and public sector. This does not mean that there needs to be all new comprehensive universities, but rather a richer diversity of programs at existing universities would create a wider network across the state and a denser concentration of newly-minted knowledge workers held in high regard by employers. Specific institutions could choose to specialize at the graduate level in particular areas. In the public sector, SUNY could create a second-tier of research universities based on a model of specialization in certain graduate-level areas. But such an expansion of higher education at the graduate level should not be based solely on a model of colleges as growth generators—they can do much for community health (Maurasse, 2001; Campbell et al, 1985). Indeed, community colleges often function to work with business and other community groups to provide practical education to students despite most having little research requirements of their faculty compared to research universities. New York needs their services.

As Pendall et al (2004:6) discuss, higher education adds to New York's economy in three basic ways:

> Higher education contributes to Upstate's economy in at least three ways: Through direct expenditures on higher education and the indirect (multiplier) effects it generates; by bringing out-of-state dollars into upstate; and by educating the future labor force. Education enhances productivity, and productivity growth is essential for economic success—especially for states like New York whose population and labor force are not growing rapidly.

Of course, economic health is a major function of higher education. More broadly, we may look at the impact of higher education on community health as involving initiatives for direct investment in community neighborhood stabilization and cultural enrichment.

Besides their educational functions and economic offshoots, some colleges and universities also invest directly in their local communities. In Ithaca, Cornell University is directly involved in real estate. Not bound to as great a degree to turning a quick profit, the university has been able to develop with an eye toward wider social benefits. One project, the Ithaca Downtown Office Project, has built a nine-story multi-use building on the Ithaca Commons. The project includes over 8,300 square feet of retail space, 30,000 square feet of office space, and 200 Cornell employees transferred downtown. A hotel is also part of the project. Similarly in Syracuse, Syracuse University has invested its own funds in the Crouse-Marshall plan. This urban revitalization plan is attempting to create a unique urban neighborhood with retail and entertainment immediately to the north of the university's main campus. To do this, the streetscape has been rebuilt with new lighting, sidewalks, sitting areas, and a new parking configuration.

It is not just large universities that make such a difference. In Hamilton, Colgate University has used its own funds and the ample resources of its alumni network to invest directly in the Central Business District. The Partnership for Community Development (PCD) is formed by two members appointed by the university's president, two by Hamilton's mayor and two by the town supervisor. Six more members come from the 'community at large': the idea is for the PCD to "represent the diversity of the area it [the PCD] serves in terms of geography, as well as economic, social, ethnic and age groupings" (PCD, 2004). A key component is Hamilton Initiative LLC, a for-profit real estate firm that buys and refurbishes downtown buildings. Its signature project is a building at the main intersection downtown that had become rather rundown. Not only did the partnership restore the building, the university moved its bookstore to the space, allowing it to become a community fixture as well as a place for students to buy books. Not only is the building restored, but the cultural offerings of the University are available for public enjoyment, whether they be public speakers or simply a good cup of cappuccino.

SUNY colleges have also participated in such efforts. At the University of Buffalo, the Urban Design Project has used faculty and student talent to design such projects as the Queen City High Regional Action Plan and the Waterfront

Initiative (Urban Design Project, 2004). At SUNY Oneonta, the Center for Economic and Community Development has been conducting research and assisting communities with their planning and economic development needs for over fifteen years.

In order to work, each campus, public and private, has addressed its unique local circumstances by reaching out to the community at large—not just government officials. They utilize the talents of faculty and students, and leverage the economic and cultural power of their respective institutions. But this resource is not utilized to its potential. Particularly in SUNY, but true with the private schools as well, there is little money available. The first priority with these schools is education—they are education institutions, after all. The creation of a state fund, external to those earmarked for education itself and thus administered outside the SUNY system and Department of Education, could create the incentives for more such programs.

Programs that promote neighborhood stabilization often involve direct investment as well. Such programs are useful not only for the residents of a community, but for the institutions as well. Perhaps one of the best examples of such a program is that of Union College in Schenectady. By the early 1990s the pain of inner city Schenectady was evident to many who visited the neighborhood, and Union College was in the middle of the mess. College officials were quietly concerned that the state of the neighborhood could impact the decision of prospective students and their parents. So, in 1998, Union started the Union-Schenectady Initiative in order to "revitalize the neighborhood to the immediate west of the historic campus and stimulate home ownership in that area" (USI, 2004). Since the program began, over forty homes in and around the college have been restored. Some buildings are used for college businesses, but others have been sold to residents. The college has financed programs to encourage more home ownership in the area. Employees of the college have access to low-interest mortgages, and even non-employees can get a good deal.

In Troy, only a few miles from Union College, the Sage Colleges are also encouraging home-ownership and revitalization of the historic homes near its riverfront campus. The program funds loans for down payments and renovations to families who wish to buy in the neighborhood, with 20 percent of the loan forgiven for each year the family stays in the home. A small grant covers legal expenses and families have access to mortgages. The children are then eligible for up to 80 percent off Sage College's tuition.

In Syracuse, the Center for Community Design and Research at SUNY ESF has been assisting with community development work, particularly from a design standpoint for years. The center provides the type of services that many communities cannot afford. Such services, combined with the type of direct involvement exhibited in Schenectady and Troy, could have a real impact on upstate communities. What's missing is not only the funding but the will to make it happen.

## Little Misses

We should not think of opportunities as always belonging to the 'big picture'. Small gestures and touches can add up to big things: missed opportunities add up too.

For instance, several years ago two hospitals in Utica—St. Luke's Medical Center and Faxton Hospital—merged. In time, Faxton Hospital was closed and with that move the exit sign on the North-South Arterial was wrong. Whereas the exit sign once read "Burrstone Road West—Faxton Hospital" the sign now has a green slab bolted over the Faxton Hospital and so reads only "Burrstone Road West". Of course, the exit leads visitors to other Utica mainstays that could have been affixed over the Faxton Hospital line, such as Mohawk Valley Community College, Roscoe Conkling Park (designed by Frederick Law Olmstead), or the Uptown business district. Our favorite would be the Utica Zoo, perhaps the city's best kept secret and an institution deserving of the higher profile its own exit would provide.

Several upstate cities have zoos, just as they all have art museums and a YMCA. In Utica, the zoo is set amidst Roscoe Conkling Park. You can view the camel while looking at sweeping views of the city, take in the sea lion show, and stroll through the woods to look at the wolves (caged, of course). It is the kind of institution that truly benefits the area, and if it was better funded could be one of the area's great attractions. Rather than invest in this jewel, however, state, county and city governments treat it as if it is an unnecessary luxury and fund it appropriately. It is an example of a "little miss:" an opportunity to create an attraction or other community institution that would increase the prestige and tourist appeal of the area that is not being utilized to its potential.

The experience of the Utica Zoo is rather typical. New York spends less than competitor states on higher education, even with its potential to revitalize communities (Pendall, 2004):

> New York appropriated just under $200 per capita, less than 33 other states. New York spends significantly less than other economic competitor states such as North Carolina ($295), Texas ($239), and California ($273).

Given this, it is not surprising that New York under funds the arts and other educational institutions. How about funds for state of the art zoos? Or decent science museums? Consider the fact that Chattanooga, Tennessee has a world renowned aquarium and yet is only the size of Syracuse. By that measure, there should be several in upstate New York. The fact of the matter is this: other regions, with less population, have more—upstate New York can too!

## Culture and Economy

New York has considerable potential to leverage its cultural resources—its history and art museums, its colleges and universities, and its other cultural institutions such as zoos—into considerable economic resources. In fact, there is most likely room for growth in these resources. Just as the economy cannot be separated from the political structure, cultural considerations, and the environment, New York's cultural resources can thrive only if we muster the political will to invest in such existing ventures as the Utica Zoo and public and private colleges and universities. Of course, such investments should be thought of as economic investments, and the location of such investments should be considered carefully.

## Notes

1. See also: Center for Community Design Research, Cornell University Real Estate Department, Crouse Marshall Revitalization Plan, and Midtown Colleges.

# Best Made Plans 7

The 2006 gubernatorial campaign was an important one for upstate New York as it made the fate of upstate a centerpiece. This was all the more poignant as the frontrunner, Elliot Spitzer, was heir-apparent for the job almost from the start. Spitzer won in a landslide, only to resign amid a scandal on March 17, 2008. Nevertheless, the rhetoric about upstate's challenges emanating from both parties since that fateful election have been illuminating.

Both parties have promised change, and it remains to be seen if New York government can rise to the challenge. Of course, change is a word not unfamiliar to upstate New York. From an economy focused on industry and agriculture to one that is now more closely related to office work and tourism, upstate residents are certainly familiar with change. Changes in the economy have brought with them changes in community and community investment (or lack thereof) as well as changes in family structure, education and healthcare.

Looking at the plans and rhetoric put forward by Republicans and Democrats one notices many similarities, some bones of contention, and quite a bit that is not so new. Both parties promise a smorgasbord for businesses large and small through tax benefits and regulatory changes. Each party addresses a particular demographic—the parties' respective "base;" while neither discuss how to pay for everything, and neither address root problems. What the parties have given us is a fine example of what happens when policy is formed in the crucible of electoral politics. Let's take a look.

## The Democrats

The Democrats in New York have nearly always found their base in the cities. This has given rise to a myth of "upstate Republicans" and "downstate Democrats," but this has never really been true. Republicans have historically run very well on Long Island, and the Democrats have historically had strong machines in upstate bastions like Albany and Utica. Not surprisingly, the Democrat plan has a tilt toward the conditions as they exist in upstate cities and the rural areas soon to be exurbs of New York City. Centered in the most prosperous region of the state, they not surprisingly question the divisions in the state and call for unity.

Since the election of Elliot Spitzer, there has been some movement on the Democrat agenda for "One New York." First on the Spitzer agenda was government reform, aimed at changing the State from one opposed to change to one that embraces change. He suggested that government reform was three-fold: campaign finance reform—including lowering contribution limits, closing existing loopholes that have allowed special interests to get around limits, as well as lowering contributions by lobbyists and in-state business interests. Ultimately campaign finance reform is not a new idea, but rather one that is often revisited because those it targets are able to find ways around the new regulations. Additional lobbying reform would ban gifts to elected officials and close loopholes in the 'revolving door' law making it more difficult for legislative employees to lobby their former colleagues for a designated time. A final effort would involve revamping the election process by creating a redistricting commission that is independent and nonpartisan to prohibit gerrymandering and to create more competitive elections.

On April 29, 2008, the New York Public Interest Research Group (NYPIRG) sponsored a rally calling on state legislators to reform state government. On its website, NYPIRG claims that New York's Ethics Laws are among the nation's weakest and campaign finance continues to be an important and largely unaddressed issue. Similarly, NYPIRG continues to argue for a constitutional amendment forming an independent commission to form assembly and senate districts. Politicians elected by and then serving individuals would seem to place all state residents, including those Upstate, in a better position to have their issues addressed and their voices heard. One aspect that needs to be addressed is the relationship between an assembly or senate seat and the population of the district. The position of "one person, one vote" is a democratic ideal that should be pursued, but it is worth noting that if implemented in both houses it would give a growing downstate an increasing share of government—upstate would, in effect, lose representation. This is not a new situation as the framers of the federal constitution faced a similar situation between protecting rights of both populous and more rustic states. In New York, a similar solution to the one followed by the federal government would be equitable: the creation of senate districts that would not change size, similar to the states, that would be entitled to two senators, and the creation of assembly districts that would change (by independent commission to prevent gerrymandering) according to population after every census. This would ensure that one house protects against the "tyranny of the majority" while the other reflects the views of the population as a whole in line with "one person, one vote."

Another topic on the Democrat's agenda for the state was restructuring the government at every level. This would begin with judicial reform—the current court system in New York is not only costly, creating a significant tax burden, but is often unsuccessful at providing justice to residents. Reform would include a more consolidated and integrated court system that limits the selection of judges to those best qualified based on merit rather than politics. In addition, democrats proposed to limit the state's public authorities by making their actions more transparent to the public while at the same time holding them accountable for their actions. Public authorities at all levels would be reviewed and eliminated if they were found no longer necessary, leaving only those who are experts selected based on their expertise rather than political favor. Regarding the third component of government reform, Democrats proposed a review of the multiple layers of local government with an eye toward eliminating those that duplicate services and thus cost taxpayers millions of extra dollars each year.

The Commission on Local Government and Competiveness was formed in 2007 and released their final report in 2008 with a variety of recommendations. According to the Commission (NYSLocalGov.org), if adopted:

- More services will be provided on a countywide or regional basis, which will both save money and provide better service. In most cases, this will be the result of a local choice to regionalize, but we will tip the balance in favor of making such choices.
- Local governments will operate under more modern, consistent, and understandable rules, and citizens will have a clearer understanding of where responsibility lies for services.
- School consolidation issues will be examined, and it will be more likely that consolidations will occur where they are fiscally and educationally advantageous.
- There will be a local conversation on how fire and emergency medical services can best be provided and the volunteer system preserved, with the likelihood that some counties will move forward with restructuring initiatives.
- Health insurance costs—a major driver of local government expenditures—will be significantly reduced statewide, and we will also address other major cost drivers such as pension contributions.
- With uniform local election days, there will be greater participation in local democracy and voters will be presented with alternatives to continuing business as usual.
- There will be better information on local finances allowing citizens to easily compare their costs for services to neighboring communities.
- We will move away from elective offices for professional functions, such as highway maintenance, giving town boards and supervisors more direct accountability and control.
- We will stimulate local demonstration projects illustrating new models for 21st century governance and encourage collaborative regional action.

Many of these are very good ideas, so good in fact that several had already been proposed by similar commissions dating back to the early 1990s. The Commission suggests a savings of nearly $1 billion per year.

Much of the concern of both parties has been the status of the upstate economy. Since the 2006 election, the democrats had favored a three-pronged approach: adjusting to the knowledge-based economy, reducing the cost structure in New York State, and significant investment in infrastructure (Spitzer, 2007).

In an effort to adjust to the knowledge-based economy former Governor Spitzer looked to education reform. He proposed to shift education concerns from those centered around money, adequacy, and what can be done tomorrow to those focused on performance, excellence and the here and now. How would such a proposal have been implemented? A school district would receive more money as long as it could show how it was spent and what kind of results were achieved, with additional awards provided to those who succeed and consequences for those who did not. School districts receiving new funds would not only show how they were used, but also apply these funds to programs that are proven to work—such as smaller class size, more time in the classroom, Internet libraries, and quality teaching. In addition to efforts in the public K-12 school districts throughout the State, the Democrats also proposed to pay close attention to children from birth to five years old—a time of critical development. With new budget realities swirling around Albany, however, the ability of the state to fund these activities is questionable.

As for higher education, the final report of the Commission on Higher Education was released in 2008 (CHE, 2008). The Commission received white papers from a number of sources and held hearings in Buffalo, Long Island, and twice in New York City; or, three hearings in the state's largest metropolitan area and one in the second largest metropolitan area. Nevertheless, most of the recommendations are quite sensible, although expensive. They include increased funding for research, faculty recruitment, and graduate programs. In addition, the report called for enhanced funding for physical and electronic infrastructure, increased aid to students by creating a low-interest student loan program and adjusting the Tuition Assistance Program (TAP) to provide more funding to the middle class. It also calls for regulatory changes in the way programs are approved and public universities are funded. Some recommendations, however, are questionable.

Under the Commission's recommendations, the SUNY and CUNY university centers would be the big winners, as noted on page 46: "The Commission has concluded that, to enhance their integral role in the State's intellectual and economic development, it is essential that SUNY's research universities receive focused attention and support." The impact on smaller colleges, in and out of the SUNY system, of the university centers' plans to dramatically increase undergraduate enrollments is not discussed in the report, for instance. Similarly, the emphasis when discussing expanding research seems oriented toward the four research university centers and specialized doctoral schools such as SUNY College of Environmental Science and Forestry and Cornell University.

A separate recommendation calls for improved transfer articulation; that is, making it easier to transfer a course such as Introduction to Sociology taken at one college in the system to another in the SUNY system. This is, of course, a good idea, but the report implies that this is a concern for public universities only, effectively endorsing a mandate that will not affect private colleges at all. To make matters worse, while it is assumed that a course entitled Introduction to Sociology (as well as others—one recommendation recently passed by the SUNY University Senate calls for all 100 and 200 level classes to fall under this rubric) is held to the same standards at all colleges. For instance, most four-year and doctoral colleges and universities require a minimum of a Masters Degree, and often a Doctorate, in the area of study to be taught. In our hypothetical example, this would require a Masters in Sociology. In practice, in many such schools this means that full time faculty have Doctorates and part-time adjunct faculty have Masters degrees in Sociology. In contrast, many two-year colleges only require the faculty member—both adjunct and full-time faculty—to hold a Masters degree in, well, something. Frequently, that something is a Masters in Education. It is worth noting at this juncture that the Commission calls for increasing full time faculty in order to increase the qualifications of those teaching such courses, in part to increase the percentage of faculty who hold doctoral degrees teaching courses. The Commission does not comment, however, on the need for two year institutions to require faculty teaching courses expected to transfer seamlessly to four year colleges to update their own credentials to those at the four year institutions. This is not to say that a faculty member with a Masters of Education is not qualified to teach the course, but the individual does not have the same training as one with a Doctorate or even a Masters degree in the specified field. Keep in mind: an award winning History professor is not only considered unqualified to teach in most positions in Education departments, but in high schools as well. Why change the standards for colleges if we won't even do so in high schools?

In essence, the Commission calls for the University Centers to receive more funds, and for the seamless transfers from two-year colleges to other colleges in the system, but it is unclear that the four-year comprehensive colleges get anything more than new mandates and the promise of continued secondary status within SUNY. More importantly, however, is the basic philosophy of the Commission: there is no attempt to restructure higher education or explore new relationships among public and private institutions; the basic structure of higher education in New York is assumed to be fine. The closest recommendation to restructuring higher education calls for the creation of "Global Science Excellence Clusters" in upstate cities. This would encourage public and private colleges and universities in certain cities to work together on particular areas of science and technology, and holds promise, but could also conceivably divert public funding from state-supported colleges in rural areas to private colleges in urban areas in the future.

Democrats have also suggested investing in basic infrastructure such as electricity and highways. As noted in earlier chapters, this is a very good idea, but it is notable that neither Democrats nor Republicans have called for the kind of investments discussed in those chapters. Plans for railroad work with the existing rail lines, and the same is true for highways.

## The Republicans

In May 2007, New York State Senator Tom Libous along with many of his colleagues announced that it was time to revitalize the economy in upstate New York. They proposed *Upstate Now*, an economic growth plan focused on job creation in the upstate area. With the support of Senate Majority Leader Joseph Bruno, they promised $3.7 billion in tax relief, investment and economic incentives over the next three years. The Chair of the Senate Committee on Commerce, Economic Development and Small Business, Senator Jim Alesi, claimed that this plan would "greatly improve the economic picture for upstate residents" (Senate Majority, www.nyfb.org, 2007).

The goals of the *Upstate Now* plan included providing opportunities for young New Yorkers as they entered the wide world of work by creating thousands of new jobs while at the same time generating economic investment in communities throughout upstate. The plan had 10 primary objectives: 1) tax relief to New York businesses; 2) improvement of Upstate's infrastructure; 3) encourage growth and innovation and technology; 4) promote energy independence and clean alternative energy; 5) reduce healthcare costs on small businesses; 6) revitalize aging Upstate communities; 7) attract new manufacturers; 8) invest in workforce preparation programs; 9) encourage entrepreneurs and 10) promote Upstate's recreational and cultural opportunities. The plan had a wide array of support from the business community, including the Business Council, the Manufacturers Association of Central New York (MACNY), the Greater Syracuse Chamber of Commerce, the Buffalo-Niagara Partnership, Greater Rochester Enterprise, the National Federation of Independent Business, and the Retail Council of New York State, all of which commented favorably regarding the plan (Senate Majority, 2007).

The coalition of business associations reflected the ultimate winner in the plan. The plan sought to reduce corporate tax rates, to simplify the complex tax code, and to reform Wick's Law. Businesses also applauded stated efforts to increase investment in the upstate economy as well as those aimed at improving infrastructure and encouraging regional partnerships, leading one to wonder who would pay for such investments. The plan proposed to eliminate business taxes on manufacturing; provide tax rebates to small businesses with fewer than 20 employees; and reduce the Corporate Franchise Tax Rate; reduce other taxes on small businesses; encourage the Federal Government to stop taxing New York's economic development incentives; and capitalize on unused investment tax credits (Senate Majority, 2007). It certainly would help current businesses, but it is debatable whether they would attract new jobs. Studies have shown that business is often more concerned with labor costs and regulations than with taxes, and neither *Upstate Now* nor the Democrat's plans can adequately address the impact of foreign competition in terms of people's incomes.

The second step in the *Upstate Now* plan promised to upgrade the current infrastructure to 21st Century standards. It includes the building of high-speed passenger trains to connect New York's cities as well as rebuilding roads and bridges in accordance with a Highway and Bridge Capital Plan. It also included the extension of broadband capabilities across the state and revitalizing water and sewer lines to support growth in suburban and rural communities. These sound more promising for the everyday taxpayer. Broadband access statewide, improved roads, bridges and high speed rail as well as up-to-date water and sewer districts would certainly benefit upstate residents (Senate Majority, 2007). The notion of being able to be connected to upstate cities quickly would make job opportunities in more places readily available to anyone who is interested. If commuting times could be decreased by better roads and bridges this too would benefit the upstate worker, particularly those in rural areas accustomed to narrow winding roads.

The next item in the plan was to make upstate more a part of the international business world by focusing on technology, research, and innovation. This step would require attracting major manufacturers in the field by granting refundable tax credits as well as $100 million made available for regional partnerships pursuing strategic investments. Investments in agribusiness and related research and technology as well as other research ventures within the State were also promised. Sales tax exemption would be available to businesses in academic incubators and commercialization assistance grants and incentives for bioscience and nanoscience commercialization. Finally, Economic Development zones would be reconfigured to address needs specific to rural areas (Senate Majority, 2007).

The fourth component of the Republican's plan involved reducing energy costs for employers and promoting energy independence. This component involved not only the promotion of energy independence but the promotion of clean alternative energy as well as energy cost assistance for some 386,000 small businesses at a cost of $350 million in the form of a refundable energy tax credit. Other tax credits would be given for solar and fuel cell manufacturing, offering ethanol production or other alternative energy use and $300 million provided for clean, renewable energy research and commercialization (including clean coal and bio-fuels). The Petroleum Business Tax would be eliminated, and low-cost power programs such as Power for Jobs would be extended, and land used for Biofeedstock Production would receive reduced property taxes (Senate Majority, 2007).

Next on the agenda was reducing health care costs for small businesses. The goal here was to make health insurance available to more families. Many families rely on the primary wage earner's employer to provide them with health insurance at a reduced rate as part of their benefit package. This component of the *Upstate Now* Plan would make it easier for small businesses with few employees to provide a health care option to their employees by enabling such businesses to purchase Healthy-NY at a subsidized cost as well as providing a tax credit for small business health insurance costs. In addition, the Healthy-NY program would be expanded to cover individuals from 208 to 250 percent of the federal poverty level. The final note for this agenda item would be exempting health savings accounts from state health insurance mandates (Senate Majority, 2007).

The *Upstate Now* plan also sought to provide money to improve central business districts throughout the state. This would involve the rehabilitation of old buildings and the clean-up of environmental hazards such as brownfields to encourage new development. In addition, they would create community renewal zones and enact an asbestos remediation credit. Finally, they would encourage the development of historical sites, the arts and recreational assets (Senate Majority, 2007).

Another point was to rebuild the manufacturing base of upstate New York. The idea was to target global manufacturers who are ready and willing to locate manufacturing facilities in the United States and develop regional incentive packages to encourage these entities to look at upstate New York by offering tax credits to major manufacturers locating here (Senate Majority, 2007). Of course, New York already does these things: one of the initial selling points of Empire Zones was that businesses in such zones have tax burdens similar to those in Alabama. If the Pataki Administration had questionable results with the zones, is the goal to have the Paterson Administration lower the tax burden to be competitive with China?

The seventh point in the plan was to prepare a workforce that is skilled and ready to move into the types of jobs that will likely become available. The plan suggested expanding remote learning opportunities through the SUNY Learning Network as well as new initiatives, including high technology high schools and assistance for employers that invest in training their employees.

The plan also called for the establishment of a One-Stop Business Start Up and Support Program. This would require a series of steps, including creating a new 5-1-1 Hotline for Small Businesses; a Virtual Business Toolbox; a Virtual Business Incubation Program; and an online clearinghouse of understandable forms and regulations. In addition, they proposed start-up funds for new businesses and the provision of revolving loan funds for business.

The final component of the *Upstate Now* Plan was to market the natural resources of the upstate region more effectively by placing a significant amount of effort on recreational and cultural tourism-oriented activities throughout upstate. This would involve improving local coordination and marketing for regionally-significant tourism destinations. The numerous historic sites and the wide breadth of cultural heritage throughout the region would be promoted, as well as agri-tourism, including farmers' markets and wine trails (Senate Majority, 2007). Tourism, whether it be through museums and other unique institutions, historical sites, nature, or culture is often the last bit of hope for many upstate communities. Overall, if done right, tourism can be good for a community, but it is not a panacea.

## Assessing the Plans

The unfortunate fact that becomes apparent upon examination of the plans put forward by both parties is that neither is willing (or able?) to live up to the rhetoric of "looking outside the box." Both parties have good ideas—new investment in basic infrastructure, technology, job training and education—but both have difficulty in explaining how to pay for such new programs. Placed well out-of-bounds are ideas that would dramatically restructure local government or alter the functioning of state agencies or of the public universities. Incremental change is in some ways worse than no change because it obscures the need for real change.

A report issued by Minnesota Senator John Hottinger addresses the issue of the state subsidies for businesses, called for in the plans of both parties, by stating that, "every year, New York's state and local governments hand out hundreds of millions of dollars in corporate subsidies." (Hottinger, DMIReport). From tax breaks and low interest loans to a variety of other development assistance, New York consistently supports corporations in an effort to create and retain jobs and promote growth. Yet the outcomes have been questionable, and upstate New York in particular suffers from significant job losses and continued economic decline. Indeed, reports from the State Comptroller's office as well as independent organizations suggest that these incentives have failed—job creation standards are often unmet. Hottinger (DMIReport) claims that one of the more effective answers to such outcomes is to spend economic development dollars more efficiently, and this can be done by legislating more transparency and accountability. Such an approach could help to ensure that communities see real benefits in exchange for business subsidies.

Hottinger (DMIReport) discusses how such a program was implemented in Minnesota. The subsidy accountability law in Minnesota, the first of its kind in the nation, lists a series of requirements for those providing business subsidies. They include uniform criteria for all deals and specific wage criteria for jobs created, public hearings for subsidies of more than \$100,000, stipulations on businesses receiving more than \$75,000 in loans or more than \$25,000 in other subsidies, job enhancement criteria or a net increase in jobs in the state within two years, and subsidies to retain jobs are only allowed if job loss is "specific and demonstrable." Those who fail must repay the subsidy with interest and may face additional penalties—they may be banned from receiving future subsidies. Businesses that receive subsidies must remain in business on the site for at least five years. All of this information must be made available to the public.

An assessment of the subsidy accountability law took place in 2003. Good Jobs First found that there was an increase in the amount of media coverage surrounding subsidy deals and these deals also became more transparent as citizens became more involved. In addition, the study found that communities sought more high-wage deals and industries used more pay-as-you-go financing rather than taking on public debt. Another study found that businesses receiving subsidies through the State's program in 2004 surpassed their two-year job creation and wage standards by 2006. There were 2,601 full-time jobs with an average hourly wage of $14.86 created during this time period. Statistics like these might make similar legislation appealing to residents of Upstate New York (Hottinger, DMIReport).

Consider the recent case of Beech Nut Nutrition Corporation. In May 2007 Beech Nut announced that it will replace two aging factories currently located in the small upstate communities of Canajoharie and Fort Plain with a new facility to be located in the town of Florida, a suburb of Amsterdam. The 356 jobs at these facilities will be retained and 135 new jobs will be created. The project will include moving the corporation's headquarters from St. Louis, Missouri to the new facility about 30 miles northwest of Albany. This project is part of a $124 million expansion in upstate New York that includes tens of millions of dollars in public grants, loans, and tax breaks. These initial funds will be spent on the construction of a 650,000-square foot processing and packaging plant and corporate headquarters (Associated Press, 2007).

It can be argued that moving a business from point A to point B in Montgomery County is not advantageous to all upstate residents—it simply moves jobs from one place to another. In this particular case subsidies are being given to an existing Upstate business. This will not necessarily improve upstate communities; in fact, in this case the small community of Canajoharie, the original home to Beech-Nut Nutrition Corporation more than a century ago, is going to lose a major employer and a mainstay of downtown for decades. Furthermore, in addition to the building subsidies, Beech Nut has been offered $18 million by the Empire State Development Corporation once job and other targets have been satisfied. These funds will cover construction, machinery, and equipment costs. Beech Nut will also be eligible for $42 million in tax breaks for moving to the Economic Development Zone. In addition, the Montgomery County Industrial Development Agency has also made a provision including $38.5 million in tax incentives. The list of incentives also includes a $2 million grant from the New York State Energy and Research Development Authority, a $750,000 grant from the state Department of Housing and Community Renewal's Office for Small Cities, $250,000 in grants from the power delivery company and a $3 million grant from the state Assembly (Associated Press, 2007).

Beech-Nut Nutrition Corporation is not the only business that has made big announcements in 2007 that will greatly impact upstate residents. General Motors Corporation announced that it will strategically phase out operations at its aging powertrain plant located in Massena by the end of 2008. This decision will result in the end of 500 jobs. This decision was based on changes in manufacturing technology that rendered the 48-year old factory obsolete, and modernization was deemed too costly. In this case there is total job loss which in the end is worse than job relocation as in the case of Beech-Nut (Associated Press, 2007). After Beech-Nut's announcement state officials commented that, "Beech-Nut's announcement is the fifteenth this year involving upstate economic development projects that . . . will keep or create nearly 6,000 jobs in Albany, Broome, Steuben, Monroe and Erie counties." (Associated Press, 2007) This sounds like good news, but how much does it cost taxpayers in the long run? If we need to pay companies, even New York companies, to stay in the state, does this not indicate a problem more serious than one or two companies looking to leave? As good as it is to see Beech-Nut stay in New York rather than leave, it seems evident that the cost of such loyalty indicates a problem bigger than Beech-Nut and General Motors put together. How sustainable is it in the long run to keep paying companies not to move?

While many politicians and corporate leaders suggest that companies simply cannot stay in New York, some do demonstrate an uncommon commitment to the state. An economic impact report published by Excellus BlueCross BlueShield in 2006 speaks of the state of healthcare in Upstate New York (Excellus, 2006). The report touts Excellus as playing a significant role in improving the health care received by Upstate residents. Indeed, they employ more than 7,000 workers with a payroll totaling $309 million making the entity one of New York's largest employers. They also take credit for spending upwards of $250 million in 2005 on direct purchases, and this figure does not include the money their employees pump into the economy. Excellus also claims that they are not only in the healthcare business but in the community business, working with the local organizations where they are located throughout Upstate New York and focusing on investment to improve not only health status but their communities' quality of life (Excellus, 2006).

So are these comments credible? Well, it is true that Excellus BlueCross BlueShield is headquartered in one of the larger upstate cities, Rochester. They also have several regional offices located in Syracuse, Elmira, Utica, Oneonta, and Plattsburgh. Their stated goals as New York's largest nonprofit health plan are to: provide affordable health care services to those in the communities they serve at a reasonable cost; focus on the poor and aged hoping to enhance their quality of life as well as their health status; and remain a committed nonprofit insurer. Excellus is also interested in remaining one of New York's largest employers, thereby keeping New Yorkers working by providing competitive wages, rewarding jobs, and benefits. It is also true that, unlike other for-profit health plans, Excellus has chosen not to outsource customer service and information jobs to overseas workers—showing their commitment to the local area; and Excellus is not only a provider of services and an employer but also a substantial consumer, from the basics like rent and utilities to medical supplies and other services. Ultimately, Excellus gives back to the community by supporting local businesses: spending $2.6 million per year at Xerox (copiers built in Webster where 8,100 people are employed); subcontracting with Hummel's Office Plus (headquartered in Mohawk) for office supplies; and Kodak (color printer and supplies costing more than $500,000) located in Rochester and employing upwards of 14,000 workers (Excellus, 2006.

In addition, Excellus BlueCross BlueShield helps the local health care industry as it pays claims for its 2 million members. In 2005 they paid 47 million claims totaling more than $3.8 billion to 110 hospitals, 18,000 providers and 60,000 pharmacies and other health care providers. On a daily basis they process in the vicinity of 140,000 claims paying on average $9.8 million for medical goods and services. Not only does Excellus contribute to the local health care industry but they also pay federal, state and local taxes, although exempt from some direct taxes. In 2005 alone, they paid $246 million in taxes and fees; included in this sum is $60 million or more in corporate income taxes. They also paid nearly $153 million to fund indigent care, graduate and medical education and other healthcare initiatives, most notably Child Health Plus through New York State's Health Care Reform Act tax. Excellus also supports a wide range of health-related community efforts in the form of one-time donations a well as long-term partnerships. Health on Wheels in the Utica Region serving adults in rural Clinton, Franklin and Essex counties, Health Careers Exploration Camps for high school students at 16 hospitals throughout Utica and the Southern Tier, Workforce Development in partnership with The Virtual College and Career Center in Syracuse, The Workforce Shortage Task Force of the Rural Health Network of Oswego County and the CNY Area Health Education Center, and Health Ministry of the Southern Tier providing services to the under or uninsured in Chemung, Schuyler, and Steuben counties, all benefit from support from Excellus (Excellus, 2006).

While there are certainly changes that need to be made in state and local government, we should remember that part of the change in upstate New York's economy is essentially cultural. Whereas in the past a company was founded not only to make money but to provide a service and/or employment in the local community, upstate's firms are increasingly just machines for making money. Simply stated, you cannot revitalize a region when its own leaders are looking for the door out.

## That's Politics

New York needs a paradigm shift. That is, while the rhetoric of decisive change that can affect New York is bandied about by both parties, a closer look at the proposed policies by both parties actually adds relatively little that is new. Two facts must be considered when looking at policies to affect change in New York State. The first is that, whether intentional or not, New York's policy makers are afraid to make the dramatic changes that would actually make a difference. And second, companies that truly have a commitment to New York State can find ways to help upstate—it takes a sense of loyalty to do so. Perhaps more importantly, politicians of both parties need to acknowledge that the system is not working for New York's benefit and commit to finding ways that it can.

# Rethinking Government 8

If New York needs dramatic change to make government more efficient and responsive to residents, as well as to lower taxes, what would such change look like? Before we can analyze an example of such a dramatic change, it helps to first consider the unthinkable: that some of the problems affecting New York as a whole and upstate in particular might be out of the purview of state and local government entirely.

## Highways

There is something curious about driving through North Carolina and Virginia. Interstate 95 works its way through this region where, after Richmond-Petersburg, Virginia, the next metropolitan area of over one million people is four states away in Jacksonville, Florida. Several of the exits are for federal highways, many of which are beautiful four lane boulevards stretching for miles under the southern sky. A New Yorker may comment to a passenger that the roads are better than many New York highways—wide, well-paved, and seemingly devoid of traffic nuisances. "Why can't New York build such nice highways?" you might ask. You might also want to ask why, say, North Carolina can't build them either—they're federal highways. In a sense, New York is building them.

The stretch of I-95 in North Carolina includes exits for eight federal highways—64, 70, 74, 158, 264, 301, 501, and 701. Two others—117 and 401—come within spitting distance. In contrast, consider New York's federal highways as seen from the interstates. On I-87, US routes 1, 6, 9, 9W, 44, and 209 come close but there are not exits for each one. These are the roads found south of Kingston. Farther upstate, routes 4, 11, and 20 also come close, as do 9 and 9W. This means that of the nine federal highways near I-87, all but three are found downstate. Similarly, of the six federal highways that cross I-90, four are in the Capital District (4, 9, 9W, and 20), with only 11 and 219 found in other parts of the state. Along I-81, only 11 and 20 come near the interstate highway,

**Table 8.1:** Federal Taxation and Spending in Ten Largest Donor States, 2005

| **State** | **Per Capita Federal Tax Burden ($)** | **Per Capita Federal Spending ($)** | **Return on Federal Tax Dollar** |
|---|---|---|---|
| New Jersey | 9,947 | 6,771 | 0.65 |
| Nevada | 8,359 | 5,849 | 0.67 |
| Connecticut | 11,563 | 8,827 | 0.73 |
| New Hampshire | 8,172 | 6,393 | 0.75 |
| Illinois | 7,844 | 6,351 | 0.78 |
| California | 8.047 | 6,725 | 0.78 |
| Delaware | 7,878 | 6,537 | 0.80 |
| New York | 8,758 | 7,521 | 0.82 |
| Colorado | 7,677 | 6,670 | 0.83 |
| Massachusetts | 9,800 | 8,684 | 0.85 |
| Average of Donor States | 8,000.605 | 7,032.8 | 0.77 |

Source: Northeast-Midwest Institute, 2008

and only 20 crosses I-88. One might dismiss such statistics as a fluke of highway construction, that rural North Carolina simply is better positioned for federal highways than more urban New York. But this pattern of federal spending favoring other states at New York's expense is well documented and quite widespread (NEMW, 2008).

As shown in Table 8.1, New York ranks eighth among federal tax "donor" states, or states that pay more to the federal government in taxes than they receive back in spending. Six of the ten largest donor states are in the northeast, including our neighbors in New Jersey and Massachusetts. Five of the top ten donor states are also among the top ten highest state tax burdens: Connecticut, Delaware, Massachusetts, New Jersey, and New York. The highest return on federal taxes paid by these donor states is the 85 cents received by Massachusetts, and the average is only 77 cents on the dollar.

In Table 8.2 we see the states that enjoy the greatest return per dollar of federal tax paid. The average return on federal taxes paid among these states is 172 percent, with both New Mexico and Mississippi receiving twice as much as they pay in. When one compares the return on federal tax paid among the 10 lowest taxed states (see Table 7 in chapter 1), six of the low tax states receive more in federal spending than they pay in taxes. In fact, all but one of those states (New Hampshire) receives a greater return on federal tax paid than does New York. Such states should have lower state taxes than New York because New Yorkers, in a sense, help pay their state taxes as well as our own.

As tempting as it is to simply blame state government for the high taxes, we should at least acknowledge that New York's status as a "donor" state contributes to a fairly high (but not the highest) state tax burden. Combined with

**Table 8.2:** Federal Taxation and Spending in Ten Largest Debtor States, 2005

| State | Per Capita Federal Tax | Per Capita Federal Spending | Return on Federal Tax Dollar |
|---|---|---|---|
| Mississippi | 4,287 | 9,027 | 2.02 |
| New Mexico | 5,162 | 10,752 | 2.00 |
| Louisiana | 4,574 | 8,815 | 1.85 |
| Alaska | 7,215 | 13,788 | 1.83 |
| West Virginia | 4,882 | 8,909 | 1.75 |
| North Dakota | 6,021 | 10,391 | 1.65 |
| Alabama | 5,436 | 9,265 | 1.63 |
| Kentucky | 5,275 | 8,308 | 1.51 |
| Virginia | 7,963 | 12,583 | 1.51 |
| South Dakota | 6,205 | 9,590 | 1.48 |
| Average of Debtor States | 5,702 | 10,142.8 | 1.72 |

Source: Northeast-Midwest Institute, 2008

high local taxes, this helps explain why taxes are so high in New York State. It was Senator Daniel Patrick Moynihan who would in the past regularly release data on New York's unfavorable federal tax situation, but it is comparatively rare to hear New York lawmakers turn into muckrakers about New York's status as a donor state today. Nevertheless, we cannot simply look to patterns of federal spending and taxation as the only reason for New Yorkers' high tax burdens: we must look ultimately to ourselves as well.

## State and Local Government

Taxes are not, as some may claim, the end all and be all of economic development. Many other factors are important as well, such as the overall education level of the population, the productivity of the workforce, the infrastructure for transportation, communications, power, and even the overall quality of life in a community. A single-minded determination to cut taxes may ultimately hurt these other factors and, in the end, be self-defeating. Instead of looking at taxes *per se*, it is more helpful to look at New York's system of governance as a whole.

One might remember from chapter two that New York's state tax burden ranks as the eighth highest in the nation, and jumped to number one in 2006 when local taxes are thrown in the mix. Some of this is the fault of state government. For instance, New York is one of only two states to split the cost of Medicaid financing with its counties, a fact that essentially pushes a state responsibility onto counties and ultimately into property tax bills. Ultimately, however, the issue is not one about specific programs or even about tax rates and services. It is about the overall amount of government, not size of government.

Consider a development project in an average suburban or rural area. It might be a new hotel off an interstate, or a small shopping center with a grocery store, or even a small amusement park. Consider the approvals that even a small project will need. A first step will be to apply to the town planning board who will then determine if site plan review is necessary. In most jurisdictions, review of the site plan will be necessary and will fall under the State Environmental Quality Review Act (SEQRA). SEQRA requires that the project be reviewed by any state agency with jurisdiction over some aspect of the project. This makes sense, as a project that will impact traffic should be reviewed by the Department of Transportation, for instance. This also goes for public health issues, including water and sewer issues, environmental issues (Department of Environmental Conservation), etc. In many cases, the lead agency will remain the town (or city) planning board, but in addition to state review, the county departments will also be involved. This often involves a certain amount of duplication as the county typically has its own health department and its own planning board, for instance. In some communities, the zoning board reviews the application in light of the zoning laws, and if need be there is also a zoning board of appeals. Not surprisingly, this maze of approvals and permits can easily take a year for a seemingly mundane project—driving the cost of a project up by thousands of dollars.

Unfortunately, the discourse surrounding this level of bureaucracy all too often falls into two camps battling past each other. On one side we have aligned business leaders and idealistic conservatives who see a confusing amount of bureaucracy—one that many local officials do not even understand—and who often call for the repeal of many of these regulations. Unfortunately, such calls either downplay or even deny the fact that such regulations typically grew out of situations where a lack of regulation had its own negative impacts: a lack of fire codes resulted in the Triangle Shirtwaist Factory Fire in 1911 in which 146 workers died, locked into the inferno by a management who chained the doors shut so the workers could not take a break. Similarly, most people prefer regulations to guarantee that sewage does not seep into their water supply or front yard. Often, the most stringent land use regulations are found in wealthy communities where residents seek a guarantee against land uses that might deteriorate their property values, such as strict zoning and historic conservation regulations. So, as many people decry the dizzying array of regulations, many prefer the protections they confer—at least in their own neighborhoods.

"Ah," cry the proponents of regulation, "we *want* regulation. We want protection." As a result of the calls to dismantle regulation, and to some degree substantial success at doing so, those who prefer to protect people and property values dig in to defend the status quo. The various levels of governance are seen as little laboratories of democracy, as it were. The special tax districts help people living outside those districts not pay additional taxes related to those districts.

Counties are viewed as necessary for the towns, towns are necessary for the people. Of course, state government is going nowhere. Lost is the opportunity to truly reform New York's system of regulation, because regulation is ultimately viewed as the problem, not a symptom of a larger problem. We propose that New York's issues with regulation and taxation are not problems in their own right, but rather symptoms of New York's system of governance. Ultimately, the problem is not government itself, but rather too many layers of government trying to perform too many of the same functions.

## A Proposal

Many of those who call to reform New York's system of governance focus on corruption. All of us should want good government, and we all know there is room for improvement in Albany just as there is in Washington. Nevertheless, the underlying assumption is that all that is wrong with New York is ultimately little more than a crisis of morality. We argue that what has evolved in New York in the past 200 years is less a crisis of morality—do you really think people in Texas or North Carolina are somehow more moral?—than a crisis of organization. We are all for clean government, but we should look at alternatives to the complex system of governance that we have today as well.

In Massachusetts, an idea that recurs every few years would involve the abolition of counties. The idea is pretty simple: most functions carried out by the counties can either be handled by the state government (such as social services) or by the individual towns (such as police protection). Where would they get such an idea? Their neighbors in Connecticut eliminated county government in 1960. In New York, the impetus for such a plan becomes evident when the sheer amount of government is noted:

> First, the legislature has set up a system that divides the entire state into 1,545 cities, villages, and towns with inflexible boundaries that cannot adapt to changing demographic and economic conditions. Second, the legislature has delegated land use planning and zoning authority to each of those 1,545 municipalities without any semblance of state standards for regional growth management. Third, by making those 1,545 municipalities highly dependent on local property taxes, the legislature has pitted localities against each other in a constant struggle over tax rateables. (Rusk, 2005, 2)

Not surprisingly, then, the idea of consolidation is not only found in Massachusetts and Connecticut, where such a plan would involve a drastic redefinition of government, but in New York as well, where such a redefinition is often framed as desirable but somehow manages to not make it into actual plans. A good example of a consolidation effort is the one that developed during the middle of this decade in Buffalo.

As we discussed in chapter 5, Buffalo has had a rough history since World War II. Still dubbed the "Queen City," this home to Frederick Law Olmsted parks and Frank Lloyd Wright homes was historically an elegant second city, a truly world class center whose legacy you can still see driving through Buffalo's neighborhoods and downtown. The city, like the county surrounding it, has been searching for ways to stem the population decline and revitalize both the city and the entire metropolitan region. The main impetus, however, for looking at consolidation began as Buffalo entered a renewed phase of fiscal crisis earlier in the decade.

In 2003, the crisis culminated in the appointment of the Buffalo Fiscal Stability Authority, normally known simply as the Buffalo Control Board. The Control Board was created by the Buffalo Stability Authority Act in 2003 as a watchdog over Buffalo's financial policies with an eye toward restructuring the city's finances (BFSA, 2007). The creation of such a board also gave an added impetus for city-county consolidation, a policy that county executive Joel A. Giambra had advocated since being elected in 1999 (Greene et al, 2005). In May of 2004 the Greater Buffalo Commission was created to explore and develop a consolidation plan, and it released its findings the following January.

The plan was an audacious attempt to redefine the city as coterminous with Erie County. An inner district, the Municipal Services District, would encompass the former city limits of Buffalo and be used for municipal service delivery and taxation. The remainder of the county would be known as the General Services District although, curiously, the existing governmental structure would not be changed—the towns would still be independent. Boosters of the plan claimed it would create the tenth largest city in the United States, but on closer examination the plan really focused on dissolving the city into county government. Greene et al (2005) identified five immediate issues with the plan:

1) The plan would require an act of the legislature to change the charter of Erie County. This also would involve a complex circuitry of elections, legislative requests, and approvals. In other words, the process itself would be quite lengthy. In order to successfully navigate the waters, for example, a majority of each municipality involved would need to approve the plan.

2) The new entity would gain no new assets, land area, or population. In a sense, all that would change is the seat of government. Not surprisingly, suburban and rural residents feared that the plan would involve them "bailing out" Buffalo's mess. In the city, some feared that expanding the government to include the entire county would water down the influence of Buffalo's African-American community as well that of other minority groups (see also NACO, 2005).

3) The governmental "crises" in the city as well as claims of financial mismanagement in the county created a sense of mistrust of both entities among voters.

4) Not surprisingly, voters were skeptical from the start. As Greene et al (2005:40) discussed, "A Zogby Poll conducted in May of 2004 found that 54 percent of City of Buffalo residents were in favor of consolidation, while only 39 percent of suburban voters favored the proposition. In all of Erie County, those in favor of a merger equaled 43 percent while those against were 45 percent. In 2001, Zogby found that nearly 50 percent of all suburban voters were in favor of consolidation, indicating an 11-point drop between 2001 and 2004."

5) Buffalo is politically unstable. This comment from 2005 is likely what led to the election of Byron Brown as mayor. The authors also cite county executive Joel Giambra's intention to not run for re-election in 2007.

The idea of regional government has not gone away in metropolitan Buffalo, but it has not materialized either. Some efforts, such as merging municipal water services and two correctional facilities (Erie County Correctional Facility and the Erie County Holding Center), have met with success. Nevertheless, challenges abound to a regional approach in both Buffalo and other upstate cities. Kathryn Foster (2001) outlines these challenges as follows:

1) Philosophical challenge: A classic conundrum in a democratic society is the advantage of smaller units of governance for conveying and implementing the popular will versus the advantages of large units for financing projects, especially large projects.

2) Political challenge: Regionalism involves the political involvement of people from differing locales, and by nature what might be appropriate at the regional level might not be appropriate at the local level. This is particularly true when attempting to get politicians from different local municipalities to agree on how to structure a regional government.

3) Governance Challenge: Regions typically have no central authority to function as the regional government. In Buffalo, Erie County seems close, but the rural towns in the southern portion of the county are not necessarily important to have in a regional government—they could easily form their own county separate from the proposed expanded city. Similarly, as Buffalo's suburbs spill into neighboring Niagara County, even the expanded city limits would not actually cover the entire metropolitan area.

4) Empirical Challenge: There is no proof that a regional government would actually work. This is in part because there are relatively few case studies of a city actually expanding its limits, although there are some, such as Miami and Dade County, Florida; Philadelphia and Philadelphia County, Pennsylvania; and, of course, New York and the current amalgam we call the City of New York. Some are recent (Miami) and some are historic

(New York and Philadelphia). All are quite different in intent, structure, and results.

Taking such considerations seriously, one can look at the situation in Buffalo and conclude 1) that a change in local governance should be aimed more broadly than simply addressing fiscal problems and the vague benefits of regional planning, and 2) once a decision to change local government has been made, it may be advantageous to rethink government from the ground up, even if that means dissolving the county as well.

## Regional Government: A Template

Buffalo presents an interesting example of a community where consolidation makes sense but the plan itself has attempted to do so without a high level of change. The question is: if one were to develop a governmental structure for Buffalo from scratch, would an enlarged definition of the city to include the entirety of Erie County be the model. Even leaving aside the issue of suburban Niagara County—which has a significant city in its own right (Niagara Falls)—an impartial observer of the portion of metropolitan Buffalo would likely cut Erie County into a northern "city" of Buffalo and a southern "Erie County." That is, Erie County would be composed of the southern rural townships while the suburban towns and cities would be merged into one large "city." The city could perhaps be divided into boroughs as in New York, such as one encompassing the former city of Buffalo, another composed of the northern suburbs of Tonawanda, Amherst and Clarence, perhaps another composed of Cheektowaga,

**Table 8.3:** Population of Expanded City of Buffalo & Proposed Boroughs, 1990 & 2006

| Boroughs | Population (1990) | Population (2006) | Composed of | Population (1990) | Population (2006) |
|---|---|---|---|---|---|
| Central Buffalo | 328,123 | 276,059 | Buffalo | 328,123 | 276,059 |
| Northtowns | 231,777 | 236,909 | Amherst | 111,711 | 116,773 |
| | | | Clarence | 20,041 | 28,041 |
| | | | Grand Island | 17,561 | 18,949 |
| | | | Tonawanda | 82,464 | 73,146 |
| Easttowns | 189,680 | 185,206 | Cheektowaga | 99,314 | 89,335 |
| | | | Elma | 10,355 | 11,238 |
| | | | Lancaster | 32,181 | 40,447 |
| | | | West Seneca | 47,830 | 44,186 |
| Southtowns | 91,800 | 97,932 | Aurora | 13,433 | 13,656 |
| | | | Hamburg | 53,735 | 56,140 |
| | | | Orchard Park | 24,632 | 28,136 |
| **Enlarged City** | **841,380** | **796,106** | | | |

West Seneca and Lancaster, and a fourth composed of the "Southtowns." The boroughs would have jurisdiction over locally important matters only, such as noise ordinances. The city as a whole would be responsible for the remainder of governance, providing such services as schools, fire and police protection, and truly regional planning. Since the expanded city would provide these services, it would be independent of any county (as in Virginia and Maryland, for instance)—it would, in effect, be the county.

As shown in Table 8.3, an enlarged city of Buffalo would have lost 45,274 residents between 1990 and 2006. In comparison, the existing city of Buffalo lost 52,064 residents during the same time period. This is because some of the townships in the metropolitan area actually gained population during the same time period—this is a population base that would have been saved under the enlarged city. In addition, the city as a whole would have room for expansion—the main reason why suburbs often grow while cities do not. Competition among the various municipalities in the metropolitan area would dissolve, and the movement of a company from the city to the suburbs would not have the tax ramifications that it currently does.

If an expanded city of Niagara Falls, including boroughs of Niagara (Niagara Falls city and Niagara town), Wheatfield, and Lewiston, were separated from Niagara County, there would be only four municipalities involved in planning for the metropolitan area as a whole: the city of Buffalo, the city of Niagara Falls, Niagara County and Erie County. (We will discuss the fate of rural towns shortly). The metropolitan area would not be under one governmental structure, and as such the government would not truly be "regional," but it would be far less complex than the dozens that exist now.

**Table 8.4:** Population of Expanded City of Binghamton & Proposed Boroughs, 1990 & 2006

| Boroughs | Population (1990) | Population (2006) | Composed of | Population (1990) | Population (2006) |
|---|---|---|---|---|---|
| Binghamton[1] | 63,500 | 55,305 | Binghamton | 53,008 | 45,217 |
| | | | (city) | 5,006 | 4,946 |
| | | | Binghamton | 5,486 | 5,142 |
| | | | (town) | | |
| | | | Dickinson | | |
| Easttowns | 12,361 | 11,427 | Conklin | 6,265 | 5,805 |
| | | | Kirkwood | 6,096 | 5,622 |
| Westtowns | 86,519 | 81,856 | Union | 59,786 | 54,563 |
| | | | Vestal | 26,733 | 27,293 |
| **Enlarged City** | **162,380** | **148,588** | | | |

[1] Ideally, the borough of Binghamton would also include a small urbanized portion of the towns of Chenango and Fenton

Such a plan of redefining the city limits for New York's metropolitan areas would work in nearly any region of over 100 thousand people. For instance, in the Binghamton metropolitan area, the city has lost almost eight-thousand people since 1990, and the metropolitan area has also consistently lost population since 1990. The urbanized core of the metropolitan area is divided among several municipalities, including both a city and town of Binghamton, the towns of Vestal, Kirkwood, Conklin, Dickinson, Chenango, and Union, and several incorporated villages. An expanded city of Binghamton would not require as many boroughs, and there would be a more severe discrepancy in population from one to another, as shown in Table 8.4.

In the Binghamton area, we have the curiosity of a suburban township (Union) that is more populous than the city itself. This is because the township contains three sizeable villages: Johnson City, Endwell and Endicott. As each community maintains separate identities, the town of Union is also home to three school districts: Johnson City, Endicott, and Maine-Endwell Central Schools. Across the Susquehanna River, the town of Vestal also has its own government and school district. An expanded city of Binghamton would thus have a western borough that would be larger than the central city borough—itself an expanded version of the former city—and the eastern suburbs would be comparatively small. Nevertheless, the enlarged city would enable regional planning, consolidated police, fire, water and sewer, and other municipal services, and an enlarged school district. The remainder of Broome County would be overwhelmingly rural, and as a rural county would be able to concentrate on issues unique to rural counties. Just as in metropolitan areas the new city governments could work on regional issues even as their constituent boroughs maintain some sense of local community control, governmental reform can allow rural counties to concentrate on their unique issues as well. But, they need to shrink.

For example, consider Montgomery County in the Mohawk Valley. The county is technically part of the Albany metropolitan area, but much of its land area is settled in rural communities or a string of small industrial towns lining the banks of the Erie Canal. The eastern portion of the county contains the city of Amsterdam and the surrounding towns of Amsterdam and Florida.

**Table 8.5:** Population of New County surrounding Amsterdam, 1990 & 2006

| Municipal Entity | Population (1990) | Population (2006) |
|---|---|---|
| Amsterdam (city) | 20,714 | 17,758 |
| Amsterdam (town) | 5,962 | 5,802 |
| Florida | 2,637 | 2,747 |
| Perth | 3,377 | 3,670 |
| **New County** | **32,690** | **29,977** |

Montgomery County as a whole, including Amsterdam, had only 49,112 in 2006, so an expanded city would not reach our goal of 100 thousand residents. Nevertheless, the city and the surrounding townships, including the town of Perth in Fulton County, are closely integrated with one another and would do well to be represented by one county government. This would allow Amsterdam to expand without competing with its suburban towns, as the city and town governments would cease to exist. As in the expanded cities, the new county would become responsible for all local services, including police and fire protection, water and sewer districts, and education. The residents of the formerly independent towns would gain access to these services, which is notable considering that many rural townships do not have a police force or, in many cases, a sewer system. In rural areas, water and sewer systems are often provided by incorporated villages or special tax districts which would, of course, cease to exist. This would also eliminate the need to maintain separate water and sewer systems only a few miles apart—under a more localized but empowered county government, the numerous small districts would become one and could be planned and expanded on a more regional basis. It would also allow residents and government in the greater Amsterdam area to concentrate on issues unique to Amsterdam—a predominantly urban county with predominantly urban issues.

In the remainder of rural Montgomery County, new counties could be formed out of closely aligned areas. Again, this would call for a new county being formed from existing townships in both Montgomery and Fulton Counties. The Gloversville-Johnstown area in Fulton County, encompassed entirely by the town of Johnstown, is tightly integrated with the Montgomery County towns of Mohawk, Glen, and Charleston. This collection of towns and cities would create a new county of almost 40 thousand residents, but the principal communities (the two cities plus the villages of Fonda and Fultonville) extend along a line from the Mohawk River to the north—a unified water and sewer district ready to happen. Fonda-Fultonville and Johnstown schools already share a swim team.

In the western portion of the county, the rural towns of Canajoharie, Minden, Palatine, Root and Saint Johnsville are marked by five major villages: Saint Johnsville, Nelliston and Palatine Bridge north the river, and Canajoharie

**Table 8.6:** Population of New County surrounding Gloversville & Fonda, 1990 & 2006

| Municipal Entity | Population (1990) | Population (2006) |
|---|---|---|
| Charleston | 1,107 | 1,326 |
| Glen | 1,950 | 2,144 |
| Gloversville | 16,656 | 15,175 |
| Johnstown (city) | 9,058 | 8,502 |
| Johnstown (town) | 6,418 | 7,237 |
| Mohawk | 3,976 | 3,954 |
| **New County** | **39,165** | **38,338** |

**Table 8.7:** Population of New County surrounding Canajoharie & Fort Plain, 1990 & 2006

| Municipal Entity | Population (1990) | Population (2006) |
|---|---|---|
| Canajoharie | 3,909 | 3,767 |
| Minden | 4,474 | 4,116 |
| Palatine | 2,787 | 3,179 |
| Root | 1,692 | 1,771 |
| Saint Johnsville | 2,773 | 2,548 |
| **New County** | **15,635** | **15,381** |

and Fort Plain on the south shore. Grouped into one county, the interests of the county would be different from the predominantly urban counties around Gloversville and Amsterdam. This would be a truly rural county, concerned primarily with rural issues such as small town revitalization, rural sprawl, and the decline of agriculture. Indeed, combined with northern Otsego County, this new county would constitute a good share of New York's Amish country. The new county would be able to concentrate its energies on rural issues in much the same way that the more urban counties and the cities would be able to concentrate on their unique urban problems. Yet, as a regional government, such services as education, water and sewer systems, police and fire protection would be available throughout. The elimination of villages and townships would enable the county to conduct regional planning and minimize competition among the various small towns in the region.

Across the state a new form of government would overtake the old. Where once there were 62 counties, now there would be perhaps three times that number of counties and independent cities, each keyed to its own local circumstances and responsive to a more narrow set of concerns. In the cities, the inclusion of suburbs in boroughs would maintain a sense of local government while the city government would handle larger issues such as planning and economic development. Gone would be separate tax jurisdictions for schools, water and sewer services, police and fire protection, and lighting: all would come under the purview of the new counties and cities. Local government would expand to include an entire community's area; counties would shrink to become truly local counties. And the tax structure would rid itself of inefficiencies that currently result in New York's burden on taxpayers being number one in the country. A business looking to expand or locate in a community would have one local government with which to discuss the issues.

State government would also have to adapt. Certain services, such as social services, Medicare, and Medicaid, would come under state jurisdiction. This would allow regional offices that could service multiple counties. In other cases, state departments that impact the same issues, such as the Department of Health, the Department of Transportation, and the Department of State which all impact the structure and ultimate health of communities, would have to consult with one another in workgroups to consider the impact of their policies. Both state and local government would be more efficient, and this should impact the dizzying array of paperwork and its expense to local businesses as well as alleviate state and local taxes. And this new structure would complete its goals without weakening the regulations that exist and, in spite of opinions to the contrary, are actually needed.

## A Long Road

Governmental reform is often a hard sell because, when push comes to shove, the thought of change is often more frightening than sticking with a system that few readily defend. Not surprisingly, it is frequently difficult to imagine a system dramatically different from the present, and as a result New York has entertained numerous proposals for change that head in the right direction but do not truly challenge the status quo. However, for change to occur, New Yorkers need to "think outside the box," as it were, and consider a governmental system as if there were not a system already in place. Once a new vision, like our own perhaps or something different, is adopted, the process of making a transition will still appear daunting but nevertheless manageable.

# I ♥ N Y 9

The ideas set forth in this book are not meant to represent the end all and be all to solving the challenges facing upstate communities.

New York, like other states, has a history of trying to solve its problems—economic, political, population, education—with a quick fix or one big project that is thought to be the one thing that will fix everything. The rationale seems to be that if this one project is a success, then there will be a trickle down effect that fixes everything else. This approach has not worked in the past and is not likely to work in the future. Even if the 'one' project was a success and provided benefits to some it is not likely to be 'the' solution to all of the issues facing upstate communities. Another favorite of those addressing upstate, whether in business, politics or basic private interests is the quick fix or band aid approach. The idea behind this approach is similar to that of the one big project approach—if one thing is fixed the others will fade into the background and the whole picture will improve. But this is not true of the human body nor of the upstate economy. If the human body is badly injured just stopping the bleeding on the surface is not likely to result in a body that is completely healed. It may make things look better at a glance, but a closer look would quickly indicate that all is not what it appears. In other words you can't always judge a book by its cover. Fixing a single upstate community or one aspect of the problem is not going to result in a revitalized prosperous upstate. Revitalizing Main Street with new sidewalks and street lights or fresh building façades may help Main Street, but is this quick fix really going to improve the entire downtown area? We need to look for the root causes of the challenges in upstate communities, and these are multiple. A decade or more of big projects and community band aids has shown us what these approaches yield. If we keep doing what we've always done we will keep getting what we've always got. Thus, providing more business incentives is not going to bring enough business to upstate to provide the number of good-paying jobs necessary to stop the college-educated from leaving upstate in search of jobs in their degree areas. Offering one more graduate program at one of our universities is not going to provide enough synergy to encourage high-tech business to locate in upstate communities. The picture of upstate is one that includes a series of tough issues that must be addressed one by one—the band aid approach helps, more jobs are created, more graduates stay, but to get the results upstate residents are really looking for more must be done. A concentrated effort of not only quality programs but programs and policies that are completely funded and carried through as proposed step by step with ample time provided before assessment takes place should at least be considered. What will work in one community may not work in another—how do we know what should/could be done? We don't. The people in these places need to have a say—they live there and know what needs to happen for change to occur.

## One More Look

To reinvigorate New York requires a holistic vision that accounts for the unique political, economic, cultural and environmental circumstances found here. Consider the environmental circumstances, for instance. To say that New York grew into the Empire State because of the advantageous position of the Hudson and Mohawk Valleys in relation to the Great Lakes would not be an overstatement. It was this position that allowed for the construction of the Erie Canal, the relative ease of the railroads to cross the Appalachians, and even for the New York State Thruway. But we should recognize that these same environmental and geographical advantages are still here, and we should safeguard them and prepare to utilize them once again. In contrast to some of the fastest growing states in the union, notably Nevada, Colorado, and Arizona, New York has access to a seemingly unlimited water supply. (But note: it is not unlimited). Given current growth rates, it is only a matter of time before the southwest, under the guise of the federal government, attempts to build a pipeline from the Great Lakes to water their growing cities. Not only should New Yorkers oppose such plans, but they should market the availability of water in New York—particularly upstate. Similarly, the availability of other natural resources, such as wind power and natural gas, should be promoted as well. Of course, tapping into such resources should be done with the local communities in mind in order to tame local opposition by treating local communities with a sense of social justice. This means, for instance, that New York should try to generate new sources of power, not simply redistribute the limited resources available. It also means finding wind turbine technology that does not mar viewscapes and waterpower technologies that can generate electricity without swallowing half a county in the process.

The social environment is as important as the natural environment. For instance, high speed rail could help both upstate and downstate communities by spreading the population over a wider area, lessoning the pressure on exorbitant downstate real estate markets while improving economic fortunes for upstate communities. A commitment to extending high speed rail to western New York could also establish prosperity throughout upstate. The advantage of rail is that it is an urban technology, and thus plays to the type of communities found in New York, large and small. By relying on suburban style technologies such as airports and highways, New York has discarded the types of community structures where it had an advantage and accepted a perceived necessity to compete against other states and countries on terms where New York has no such advantage. We might look to many European countries where a commitment to older communities, inner cities and public transportation exists next to the new technologies such as air travel and the automobile to find a different model that continues to work well. Similarly, New York cannot compete against countries where education and health care standards are so low that wages are a fraction of those in New York without dramatically impoverishing our own population. Assuming that most New Yorkers want to make more than 50 cents per hour, New York once again should play to its strengths: invest in health care, education, and even recreation to give New Yorkers the highest quality of life in the world. Although it might seem contrary to received wisdom, building communities in which people like to live is a good economic development strategy as well (Clavel & Kleniewski, 1990).

Building great places to live is also a function of utilizing New York's vast pool of cultural resources to our advantage. Education is a key component to revitalizing New York. New York can be one of the great regions for new technology in the world—it would not be a new role for the Empire State—but this involves creating the type of environments where innovation can blossom. This involves fostering the types of environments in which entrepreneurially minded people—the group Richard Florida (2004) refers to as the "Creative Class"—thrive. Through investment in education, a high level of creativity can be fostered, but without a similar effort to create communities with a high quality of life, our universities will turn out a population looking to move "where the excitement is." In other words, the local zoo, the art gallery, the natural history museum, and other cultural institutions are important, and they should be readily available to residents all over New York.

Economic reforms are necessary as well. As members of both political parties agree, Wick's Law reform is important, and other such regulations could use another look as well. New York does seem to have considerable red tape aimed at the business community, and taxes are quite high. There is room for such reform, although we should be careful not to simply eliminate such regulations without considering why they came into existence to begin with. Few people want to do away with sensible environmental regulations, and the scrapping of the social safety net would not only hurt those at the bottom but in time all New Yorkers. Nevertheless, many processes can be simplified and one suspects a number of regulations changed.

Ultimately, it is the political structure of New York that inhibits reform. We have proposed an outline of how to restructure local government, although it hardly constitutes a full-blown program of action. Ultimately, these are discussions that need to take place in Albany and in the cities and towns all over the state. The first step, however, is not to reform local government or state government; it is to admit that we need to change.

## No Easy Answers

New Yorkers need to look rationally at the state of the state. All too often, we hear emotional pleas about the plight of a particular industry and the suggestion that all we need to do is turn back the clock. It is okay to be emotional; it is right to hope and pray to save our communities. To do it, however, we need to put our emotions in check and try to objectively see the world in which New York now exists. With this in mind, we need to consider the following four general factors.

1. The issues affecting New York are complex, and we need to recognize that times have changed. Consider the discussion of deindustrialization in Utica. While it might be tempting to point to free trade agreements or taxes to explain what happened there, the issues are more complex than that. The factories were bought out by out of town firms that saw them as mere factories, not community institutions. The lack of commitment to Utica on the part of the owners allowed them to close the factories and move the product line to other states without a deep sense of regret. This is not only an economic consideration, this is a cultural consideration. In Buffalo, the closing of Bethlehem Steel in Tonawanda was partially due to the exact same scenario—the business was headquartered out of town and its owners had little regard for Tonawanda itself. Tonawanda helped the decision by inconsistent tax policies as well. Or consider the more general discussion of New York's choice of suburbanizing technologies over older urban-centric technologies. It was not just a New York phenomenon, but part of a larger cultural phenomenon that declared the car to be king. Ample money was made available by the federal government for interstate highways, and New York was able to get funds for existing highways as well as new ones. The federal government nudged the airline industry in one direction by regulating it, and New York responded not only with an airport in every metropolitan area, but sometimes more than one. Both Buffalo and Niagara Falls built airports, as did Albany and Schenectady, and curiously both Oneonta and Sidney. These technologies favored suburban locations, and for the

most part still do. When the federal government deregulated airports, the less competitive airports faced hard times, and smaller metropolitan areas now typically have sub-standard or non-existent air service. To fix the problem, either the federal government needs to re-regulate the airlines or the state needs to offer a truly competitive alternative. Otherwise, smaller cities—upstate cities—are at a considerable disadvantage.

2. So called Band-Aid approaches do not work, even if they appear to have short term benefits. There is no easy fix to New York's issues, and indeed the root causes of the problems should make it clear that we need a more comprehensive approach. While we might acknowledge that the presence of unique institutions—SUNY Oneonta and Hartwick College—in Oneonta make a major difference between the state of that city vis-à-vis Little Falls, they were not the only difference. The location of Oneonta away from a major metropolitan center forces the city to act as one itself, even if the town's population does not immediately imply such a status. But even if the presence of unique institutions were the only difference between the cities, is it really a workable policy solution to simply build such institutions in every community of more than 10 thousand residents? Clearly, we need more study. As academics, we are quite happy to see an expansion in the higher education system of the state. That said, we need to be careful not to create too much of a good thing. What makes unique institutions unique is that they are, well, unique. An analogous situation is seen in the casino industry in New York. The currently small number of casinos and similar ventures in the state attract hundreds of thousands of visitors a year to those communities. Those communities, such as Verona, home of Turning Stone Casino and Resort, experience growth as a result. The growth in Verona does not, however, imply that building casinos in a dozen more communities will spur more growth—it will likely just water down the market. The point is that to the degree that a unique institution can help a community, it can do so only to the degree that it serves a unique niche. There might perhaps be more than one community with that niche—New York can sustain many tourist towns, college towns, and even casino towns—but simply finding a policy that seems to work in one place does not mean it will work in others. Each community needs to find what is unique to itself, not merely copy the "best practices" of another.

3. Empower local communities even as we reform local government. A small number of elected officials do not know best—the community knows best. Any attempt to revitalize a community should thus involve from as early a stage as possible efforts to bring in the creative energy and potential concerns of the people who live in the community. One great way of doing this is through a process called visioning. Visioning involves town hall like meetings that are meant to create ideas and excitement about the future of a community. Typically, visioning will involve a series of meetings with the public intended to find out what residents like about their community and what type of community they would like to live in in the future. In the early stages, residents are simply asked what they like about the community, and these ideas go on the board. These ideas are then grouped into themes, and these become the focus for the next meeting. By the end of the series of meetings, the ideas of the townspeople have been refined into a vision of what the town should be like in, say, 2030, and then discussions of how to achieve these goals result in the legislation needed to get there. The empowering of local communities should be seen as a guaranteed avenue to success. The prevailing ideas that people have are shaped by the times in which they live, and sometimes people dream of achieving some goal only to find it not worth the cost in the end. For instance, in a number of upstate communities, some residents will consider an automotive speedway as a desirable route to economic development. If successful in attracting a speedway, however, some residents might find themselves complaining about the noise and traffic associated with automotive racing. In Cooperstown, for instance, the serene beauty of the village conceals a cultural conflict between two alternative images of the village: the "Historic Cooperstown" model versus the "Baseball Town USA" model. Even as successful a tourist town as Cooperstown is, there are still issues that are left to be resolved. And to some degree, this means that every new development project is bound to have detractors.

4. The fourth issue to consider relates to New York's position vis-à-vis the rest of the country. New York is the third largest state in the nation, and to some degree has a tradition of looking out for itself as a result. However, New York also has much in common with neighboring states and, more regionally, with Midwestern states. Certain ideas we have mentioned, such as high speed rail as an alternative to airlines and cars, could be quite workable in New York alone. They might be particularly powerful policies when pursued

with other states in the region. Nevertheless, a powerful regional alternative might not work in conjunction with western states, for instance, where cities are considerably farther apart than in the northeast, or in southern states, where the population is simply lower. New York should look for opportunities to work with other states in the region to achieve the policies that need to be implemented but are not being addressed by the federal government. In addition, New York's legislative delegation needs to consider themselves as New Yorkers first, as residents of our region second, and as members of a political party after these. Some policies promoted by both political parties might help some areas of the country but hurt New York—NAFTA is a good example of this. Legislators from New York should stand firm in promoting policies that are of ultimate benefit to New Yorkers and other states in our region. A good place to start would be the significant disadvantage that New York has suffered in federal tax policy and spending for decades. As other states in the Northeast and Midwest are similarly disadvantaged, there should be lots of help.

## A Healthy State

Besides the humanitarian reasons, why care about the fate of upstate? If you do not live upstate, does it really impact you? We should consider the impact of a lagging upstate as time goes on because, as the governor's plan states, in reality we are "one New York."

A lagging upstate will, in the future, become a considerable drain on the state economy—and ultimately the downstate economy as a whole. If current trends are allowed to continue, New Yorkers can look forward to increasing medical bills per capita as the state's population ages. This can already be seen as younger workers leave the state in search of greener pastures and leave their parents behind to collect Medicare and other services. This creates an imbalance in the state's economic system where a lower number of workers must support a growing number of seniors. In time, this will involve increasing payments downstate—where the younger workers are—to pay for retirees upstate. Keeping a healthy upstate economy, and the younger workers to staff it, will minimize this pressure.

The relative decline of upstate will have an impact on state politics as well, even beyond the historical rift. One needs to consider the political effects found in other societies in decline to consider the implications of a weakened upstate. Economic decline forces people to move—this is why upstate metropolitan area populations are as miserable as they are—and this causes social dislocation.

Children move away from their parents, or perhaps they stay and recognize their decision as a mistake. The political instability could, as in other countries, lead to an increasing willingness to consider political radicals, those willing to pit one region against another, even one person against another.

In contrast, a healthy upstate creates a large market for downstate goods and services that expands—close to home. A healthy upstate could expand the opportunities for innovation and entrepreneurialism; it could be a catalyst for new technologies, new art forms, and new ideas of global significance. Besides business opportunities, the possibilities in terms of cultural enrichment, for recreational opportunities beyond the metropolitan area, becomes wide open. Imagine the fun of taking a cruise down the Erie Canal if you were met with dynamic cities and towns along the way. Imagine rounding out a day of hiking with dinner and drinks found in well-preserved mountain towns. Imagine not only being able to travel anywhere in New York State in only an hour or two, but actually wanting to. Just imagine.

# Appendix

The data on changes in the composition of central business districts in Oneonta, Little Falls, and Cooperstown in chapters four and five was collected in the following way. A list of addresses in each downtown area was assembled. In Oneonta and Little Falls, the business at each address was collected by referencing city directories for each community at approximately five year intervals, where available. In Cooperstown, where city directories did not exist, data was collected for each year at two-year intervals beginning in 1987 utilizing lists supplied by the Cooperstown Chamber of Commerce and permit applications supplied by the Village of Cooperstown. Each business recorded was then coded according to the scheme outlined below. For earlier years, interviews with local residents and members of the business community were interviewed and their answers compared and recorded.

Businesses classified as "general" sell goods that are of use to the general population on a regular basis. This definition is inclusive of grocery, pharmaceutical supply, and other such general merchandise. Such businesses often sell items related to tourism, but the primary purpose of such stores is the sale of general merchandise. General stores that supply automotive fuels are designated "General-Fuel" (Thomas, 2003, 163-4).

Specialty stores sell goods that are intended for aesthetic or symbolic use, such as works of art or souvenirs. Boutiques that sell clothes in addition to a number of other specialty items were classified as specialty stores, although the store selling only clothes is classified "general." Businesses which do not have as a primary orientation baseball related merchandise were classified "specialty, non-baseball." A "Specialty, baseball" designation is applied to those stores that do have a primary orientation toward baseball related items (Thomas, 2003, 164).

Food Service establishments include businesses whose primary purpose is the preparation and service of food for consumption (Thomas, 2003, 164).

Local (and General) Services include businesses whose primary purpose is to provide a specific service, such as financial services, real estate, or minor production services such as printing, photocopying, or customer service.

A sixth category—art galleries—was also coded.

Bars and taverns were coded separately from food service establishments. In addition, adult oriented retail outlets, such as "head shops," were also separately coded. Similarly, amusements, such as pool halls and movie theaters, were given separate codes.

Civic institutions, such as the Post Office, city offices, and the offices of non-profit community groups (such as Opportunities for Otsego) were classified as "civic." Private clubs, such as the Elks Club, were classified as Private Clubs.

Car dealers and automobiles service shops were classified under "Car/Implement Dealer." Manufacturing and milling was classified under "Industrial," whereas warehousing was classified separately.

# References


Amtrak. 2007. *Amtrak.* http://www.amtrak.com.

Arndt, K. J. R.. 1937. John Christopher Hartwick, German Pioneer of Central New York. *New York History, 18, 293-303.*

Aquila, R.. 1977. *The Iroquois Restoration: A Study of Iroquois Power, Politics, and Relations with Indians and Whites*. Ph.D. Dissertation, Ohio State University.

Associated Press. 2007. *Beech-Nut to expand in Upstate NY.* www.boston.com/business/articles/2007/05/15/beech_nut_to_expand_in_upstate_ny//

Bean, P. A..1994.The Irish, the Italians, and Machine Politics. *Journal of Urban History, 20, 2, 205-239.*

Birdsall, R.. 1925. *The Story of Cooperstown*. New York: Scribner's.

Bluestone, B. & Harrison, B.. 1982. *The Deindustrialization of America.* New York: Basic Books.

Buffalo Fiscal Stability Authority. 2007. *Website.* http://www.bfsa.state.ny.us.

Campbell, Lewis B., Mason, J. Barry, Mellichamp, Joseph M., & Miller, David M.. 1985. Unlikely Partners: Company, Town, and Gown. *Harvard Business Review, 63, 20-24.*

Center for Community Design Research (CCDR). 2004. *Website.*<<http://fla .esf.edu/CCDR/home.htm>>

Christman, H. 1945. *Tin Horns and Calico: A Decisive Episode in the Emergence of Democracy*. New York: Henry Holt & Company.

Clarke, T. W.. 1952. *Utica, for a Century and a Half.* Utica, N. Y., Widtman Press

Clavel, Pierre & Kleniewski, Nancy. 1990. *Space for Progressive Local Policy: Examples from the U.S. and 1990 the U.K.*. In J. Logan and T. Swanstrom (eds.) *Beyond the City Limits*.Philadelphia: Temple University Press.

Crisafulli, V.. 1960. *An Economic Analysis of the Utica-Rome Area.* Utica, N. Y.: Utica College.

Cornell University Real Estate Department. 2004. *Projects.* http://132.236.67.165/cure/projects.htm#OP

Cooper, James Fenimore. 2007. *The Pioneers*. New York: Signet Classics.

Cornog, E. 2000. *The Birth of Empire: DeWitt Clinton and the American Expe rience, 1769-1828*. New York: Oxford U. Press.

Crouse Marshall Revitalization Plan (CMRP). 2004. *Crouse Marshall Revitalza tion Plan*. http://govt-comm.syr.edu/reports/marshall.html

Daniels, T.. 1999. *When City and Country Collide: Managing Growth in the Metropolitan Fringe*. Washington, D. C.: Island Press.

Dietz, Richard. 2007. *A Brain Drain or an Insufficient Brain Gain?* Buffalo, N.Y.: Federal Reserve Bank of New York.

Dillaway, Diana. 2006. *Power Failure*. Amherst, N. Y.: Prometheus Books.

Dressel, Andrew. (1999). *MapInfo*. Proceedings of the Computer Consultant Support Program Conference, 16 November 1999. <http://ccsp.cites.uiuc .edu>; 15 February 2004.

Ellis, D. M. 1946. *Landlords and Farmers in the Hudson-Mohawk Region, 1790-1850*. Ithaca, N. Y.: Cornell U. Press.

_____. 1979. New York: State and City. Ithaca, N. Y.: Cornell U. Press.

Ellis, D. M., Frost, J. A., Syrett, H. C., & Carman, H. J.. 1957. *A Short History of New York State*. Ithaca, N. Y.: Cornell U. Press.

Ellis, D. M. & Preston, D. M.. 1982. *The Upper Mohawk Country: An Illstrated History of Greater Utica*. Woodland Hills, Ca.: Windsor Publications.

Excellus. 2006. *Contributing to a Health Econom for Upstate New York: Economic Impact Report 2006*. www.excellusbcbs.com/download/files /economic_impact.pdf.

Federation of Tax Administrators. 2006. *State Comparisons*. http://www.tax admin. org.

Fischer, J. R.. 1997. *A Well-Executed Failure: The Sullivan Campaign against the Iroquois, July-September 1779*. Columbia, S. C.: U. South Carolina Press.

Florida, Richard. 2004. *Cities and the Creative Class*. New York: Routledge.

Foster, Kathryn, A. 2001. *Regionalism on Purpose*. Cambridge, Ma.: Lincoln Institute of Land Use Management.

Greene, Vernon, Feulner, Jason, Hautier, Julien, & Ben Walsh. 2005. *The Fu ture of Government Consolidation in Upstate New York*. Syracuse, N. Y.: Syracuse 20/20.

Goldman, Mark. 2007. *City on the Edge*. Amherst, N. Y.: Prometheus Books.

Gould, S. J.. 1989. The Creation Myths of Cooperstown. *Natural History, November, 14-24*.

Graymont, B.. 1990. *The Iroquois in the American Revolution*. Syracuse, N. Y.: Syracuse University Press.

Hottinger, John, Senator MN. 2007. *Accountability for Economic Development Subsidies*. Drum Major Institute for Public Policy. www.drummajorinstitute.org/ library/report.phpIdD=48.

Kay, J. H.. 1998. *Asphalt Nation: How the Automobile took over America and How we can take it Back*. Berkeley, Ca.: U. California Press.
Kehoe, A. B.. 1992. *North American Indians: A Comprehensive Account*. Second Edition. Englewood Cliffs, N. J.: Prentice Hall.
Killeen, Kieran M. & John Sipple. 2006. *Upstate School Reform: The Challenge of Regional Geography*. Washington, D.C.: Brookings Institution.
Kimes, Beverly R. 2004. *Pioneers, Engineers, and Scoundrels*. New York: SAE International.
Larkin, F. D.. 1998. *New York State Canals: A Short History*. Fleischmanns, N. Y.: Purple Mountain Press.
Levine, P.. 1985. *A. G. Spaulding and the Rise of Baseball*. New York: Oxford U. Press.
Logan, John & Swanstrom, Todd. 1990. *Beyond the City Limits*. Philadelphia: Temple U. Press.
Mann, Michael. 1986. *The Sources of Social Power, Vol. 1*. New York: Cambridge U. Press.
MapInfo. (2004). *Website*. <http://www.mapinfo.com>; 14 February 2004.
Markusen, A.. 1987. *Regions: The Economics and Politics of Territory*. Totowa, N. J.: Rowman & Littlefield.
Maurrasse, David J. 2001. *Beyond the Campus: How Colleges and Universities form Partnerships with their Communities*. New York: Routledge.
Middlekauff, Robert. 2007. *The Glorious Cause*. New York: Oxford U. Press.
Midtown Colleges. 2004. *Neighborhood Revitalization: Midtown Colleges and University Study*. http://www.albanyny.org/business/econdev/midtown.asp
Mills, C. Wright. 1959. *The Sociological Imagination*. New York: Oxford U. Press.
Mintz, Max M. 2002. *The Seeds of Empire*. New York: New York U. Press.
National Archives. 1998a. Fort Stanwix Boundary Line Treaty. National Archives Microfilm Publication No. 668: Ratified Indian Treaties; 1722-1868, No. 7 frame Nos. m=0138-142, pgs. M-5. Washington, D. C.: National Archives & Records Administration.
_____. 1998b. Treaty of Fort Stanwix. Fort Stanwix Boundary Line Treaty. National Archives Microfilm Publication No. 668: Ratified Indian Treaties; 1722-1868, No. 9 frame Nos. m=0152-153, pg. m-5, P=0148-151, pg. m-4. Washington, D. C.: National Archives & Records Administration.
Northeast-Midwest Institute. 2008. *Website*. http://www.nemw.org/.
New York State Department of Economic Development. 2000. *New York State Data Center*. <http://www.nylovesbiz.com/nysdc/default.asp; accessed 17 March 2003>.
Parsons, Talcott. 1951. *The Social System*. New York: Free Press.
Partnership for Community Development (PCD). 2004. *Homepage*. http:// www .partnersatwork.org/

Pendall, Rolf. 2003. *Upstate New York's Population Plateau: The Third-Slowest Growing 'State."* Washington, D.C.: Brookings Institution.

_____. 2003. *Sprawl without Growth: The Upstate Paradox*. Washington, D.C.: Brookings Institution.

Pendall, Rolf, Drennan, Matthew P.& Susan Christopherson. 2004. *Transition & Renewal: The Emergence of a Diverse Upstate Economy*. Washington, D.C.: Brookings Institution.

Pendall, Rolf & Susan Christopherson. 2004. *Losing Ground: Income and Po verty in Upstate New York: 1980-2000*. Washington, D.C.: Brookings Insti tution.

Phillips, Kevin. 2003. *Wealth & Democracy*. New York: Broadway.

Pula, J. S. & Dziedzic, E. E.. 2005. *New York Mills: The Evolution of a Village*. Syracuse, N. Y.: Syracuse U. Press.

_____. 1991. *United We Stand: The Role of Polish Workers in the New York Mills Textile Strikes, 1912 and 1916*. New York: Columbia U. Press.

Rusk, David. 2005. *Upstate New York: A House Divided*. Paper Presented at the New York Thruway Alliance Economic Summit, Syracuse, New York, May 20, 2005.

Savas, Theodore P. & J. David Dameron. 2006. *Guide to Battle of the American Revolution*. El Dorado Hills, Ca.: Savas Beatie.

Schwarzlose, R. A.. 1980. The Nation's First Wire Service: Evidence Support ing a Footnote. *Journalism Quarterly, 57, 4, 555-62.*

Senate Majority. 9/26/2007. Senate Majority launches "Upstate Now" – a comprehensive job growth and economic development plan for Upstate. New York Farm Bureau. www.nyfb.org/UpstateNow.htm.

Sheehan, R.. Dec. 1949. Take Utica, For Instance. *Fortune, 126-130.*

Spitzer, Elliot. 01/03.2007. *State of the State Speech*. New York State of the State Address 2007. www.stateline.org/live/details/speech?contentId=168384.

Springwood, C. F.. 1996. *From Cooperstown to Dyersville: A Geography of Baseball Nostalgia*. Boulder, Co.: Westview Press.

Statistics Canada. 2006. *Statistics Canada*. http://www.statcan.ca.

Taylor, Alan. 1996. *William Coopers's Town*. New York: Vintage.

_____. 2007. *The Divided Ground*. New York: Vintage.

Taylor, Monique. 2002. *Harlem: Heaven or Hell*. Minneapolis: U. Minnesota Press.

Tax Foundation. 2007. *Tax Foundation*. http://www.taxfoundation.org.

Thomas, A. R.. 1998. *Economic and Social Restructuring in a Rural Communty*. Ph.D. Dissertation: Northeastern University.

_____. 2003. *In Gotham's Shadow: Globalization and Community Change in Central New York*. Albany: SUNY Press.

_____. 2005. *Gilboa: New York's Quest for Water and the destruction of a Small Town*. Lanham, Md.: University Press of America.

Thomas, A. R., Thalheimer, J., Cook, M., & Malfitani, P. 2003. *Economic Activ ity in Downtown Cooperstown, 1979-2003*. Oneonta, NY: SUNY Center for Social Science Research.

Thomas, A. R., Dai, P. A., & Martin, S.L. 2005. *Rural Retail Redux: Supermar ket Pricing in Rural Central New York*. Oneonta, NY: SUNY Center for Social Science Research.

Thomas, A. R., Smith, P. J., Dai, P. A., Coletti, S. & Coletti, V. 2008. *Accom modations and Retail in Greater Cooperstown, 1987-2007*. Oneonta, NY: SUNY Center for Social Science Research.

Trigger, Bruce C. The Mohawk-Mohican War, 1624-1628. *Canadian Historical Review 52 (September, 1971) 3.*

Union Schenectady Initiative. 2004. *Overview*. http://www.union.edu/ Community/USI/

United States Bureau of the Census. 2006. *Quarterly Summary of State and Local Government Tax Revenue*. http://www.census.gov/govs/www.qtax.html.

United States Bureau of the Census. 2007. *American Factfinder*. http://www.census.gov.

United States Bureau of Labor Statistics. 2001. *National Employment, Hours, and Earnings*. <http://stats.bls.gov/ceshome.htm>; (accessed 3 January 2001).

_____. United States Bureau of Labor Statistics. 1984. *Employment, hours, and earnings, States and Areas, 1939-82*.

United States Library of Congress. 31 May 1779. George Washington Papers at the Library of Congress, 1741-1799: Series 4. General Correspondence. 1697-1799. Letter from George Washington to John Sullivan, May 31, 1779.

Urban Design Project. 2004. *Home*. http://www.urbandesignproject.org/

Wachs, M. & Crawford, M. (Eds.). 1992. *The Car and the City: The Automobile, the Built Environment, and Daily Urban Life*. Ann Arbor, Mi.: U. Michigan Press.

Walsh, J. J..1982. *Vignettes of Old Utica*. Utica, N. Y.: Utica Public Library.

Watts, Steven. 2006. *The People's Tycoon*. New York: Vintage.

Weber, Max. 1947. *The Theory of Social and Economic Organization*. Talcott Parsons, Ed. New York: Free Press.

Weeks, P. A.. 1981. *History of Hartwick (Village and Town)*. Richfield Springs, N. Y.: Heritage Press.

# Index

www.ingramcontent.com/pod-product-compliance
Ingram Content Group UK Ltd.
Pitfield, Milton Keynes, MK11 3LW, UK
UKHW021034150926
475561UK00003B/99

9 780761 845003